Lord
I Believe

Brian Byrne

AB ASPECT Books
www.ASPECTBooks.com

World rights reserved. This book or any portion thereof may not be copied or reproduced in any form or manner whatever, except as provided by law, without the written permission of the publisher, except by a reviewer who may quote brief passages in a review.

This book is sold with the understanding that the publisher is not engaged in giving spiritual, legal, medical, or other professional advice. If authoritative advice is needed, the reader should seek the counsel of a competent professional.

Copyright © 2013 ASPECT Books
ISBN-13: 978-1-4796-0093-9 (Paperback)
ISBN-13: 978-1-4796-0094-6 (ePub)
ISBN-13: 978-1-4796-0095-3 (Kindle/Mobi)
Library of Congress Control Number: 2013905309

Published by

Table of Contents

Introduction	The Search for Faith	v
Chapter One	Out of the Shadows	11
Chapter Two	The Faith	16
Chapter Three	Who Is He?	29
Chapter Four	Believing Into the Word of God	38
Chapter Five	Repent and Believe	50
Chapter Six	God of the Impossible	60
Chapter Seven	Obstacles	71
Chapter Eight	The Problem of Doubt	82
Chapter Nine	Conformed to the Image of Christ	89
Chapter Ten	Faith for a Pilgrim	102

Introduction

The Search for Faith

Interview between Teresa Thevenard (reporter) and Brian Byrne (author). Although this interview is fictional the facts about the author's search for faith revealed through the conversation are real.

Teresa Thevenard: Your publisher tells me you're writing a book.

Brian Byrne: Actually, it's a second book. The first was a record of a personal search to know what it meant to be the Lord's disciple in the first century.

Teresa Thevenard: And the second book?

Brian Byrne: It will cover the search to discover what it means for a pilgrim to live by faith. The two books are supposed to go together. I can't be His disciple unless I know how to live by faith. I've called the book "Lord I Believe." Like the first book, it comes out of a very personal search.

Teresa Thevenard: Thank you Brian. Speaking with you about something so personal is like delving into the inner secrets of a man and his relationship with the unseen. Can you tell me when your search for faith began?

Brian Byrne: I must have been only sixteen or seventeen when my parents and younger brother discovered Jesus. Their interest in religion bothered me. I felt like I was being confronted with an unseen world of faith that I knew nothing about and wanted to protect myself from it. I would either just not go to church, or I would make some foolish excuse for staying home. I remember one time, I used the excuse that my shoes were not polished. Even if I did go to our little country church I would refuse to enter. Instead, I would rather sit outside and wait for church to be over. Even though my parents could see right through me, they never once tried to challenge me. I didn't realize that the Lord Himself was calling me to faith. I was so full of teenage arrogance and pride that I couldn't hear Him.

Teresa Thevenard: I know what you mean. I have been there before. How long did that rebellion last? It was a kind of gentle rebellion, wasn't it?

Brian Byrne: There certainly wasn't anything violent in my refusals. Gentle would describe it, but also obstinate. This rebellion lasted around two years. I remember writing to my mother during that time and telling her that I was going to live by my own integrity. Looking back, I was a little blind and arrogant. Or maybe I was just self-reliant? She never responded to my blindness, but the Lord caught up with me. He always does.

Teresa Thevenard: When? Where? Tell me about it. So your search for faith ended?

Brian Byrne: In the same moment, it both ended and began. It's been going on ever since. In my mind's eye, I can still see the place where I asked Him to come into my heart. I was expecting some kind of miraculous sign. There wasn't any; but the miracle happened anyway. Over the next few days I experienced an unexpected, wonderful joy and delight in reading the Psalms as though they were songs of worship. It felt like there was a song inside of me singing to the Lord. Does that make sense? I can't explain it any better than that. Looking back, I like to use Peter's words to describe what was happening to me, "Joy unspeakable and full of glory."

Teresa Thevenard: You said your search for faith ended when you became a Christian. But surely your faith continued as you learned to live a Christian life?

Brian Byrne: Certainly I trusted Him that night when He became part of me. And in the days following, trust was there in my worship, but it was a short lived glory. So quickly it faded. It was when I was invited to be part of a church that I found belonging and service. I taught in the church school and began to think about serving the Lord overseas as a teaching missionary. However, the song I had known inside of me gradually faded and then stopped singing altogether. And the great sadness, Teresa, was that I didn't realize I had lost my song to the Lord. There were plenty of church activities, programmes and service, but no joy. Lots of satisfaction about what I was doing as well as the approval of my pastor and fellow Christians, but the song didn't sing any more.

Teresa Thevenard: That's sad!

Brian Byrne: Sad but avoidable. I lived for fourteen years like that. I served on two Aboriginal missions, spent one year deeply involved in another local church, three years in India, two years in New Guinea, and then another three more years in India as an educational missionary. From an outside point of view it probably looked as if I have done everything right. However, when I look back I like to think of that time as living in a grey fog. On the surface, and apart from some minor indiscretions, it was as righteous as any Christian could wish, but I must have been like Paul's description of people in the last times as, "having a form of godliness but denying its power." I think that about sums me up in those years.

Teresa Thevenard: And your search for faith?

Brian Byrne: It stumbled to a halt. What had begun so promisingly when He found me quickly ground to a halt. No fanfare or trumpets telling me what I had lost. Just silence of the spirit in the muddled noises of religious activity.

Teresa Thevenard: But surely your faith didn't die?

Brian Byrne: No, my faith didn't die. My trust had died.

Teresa Thevenard: You need to explain that.

Brian Byrne: Forgive the little lecture, Teresa. I learned that the word "faith" has two forms. The noun form and the verb form. For me the faith, the noun form, had plenty of substance, though some of that substance I have since found to be suspect. I knew my Scriptures. I had been well taught about the cross, sin, repentance, salvation, and His coming again. But the verb form was inactive. I didn't know that He was expecting me to trust Him. And I didn't know what trusting Him really meant.

Teresa Thevenard: Go on.

Brian Byrne: And another thing I didn't know at the time, is that I can't be pleasing to the Father unless I trust Him. The writer to the book of Hebrews said that. I am embarrassed to think about how much I have displeased Him during those years of my wandering in the wilderness. It's a measure of His love and tender patience that He did not once rebuke me. He waited until desperation set in and I came back to the search for faith that had been absent in my life for so long. It's not only trust or faith that has been important for me, Teresa. It's also the search, and that has to be with all my heart, soul, mind, and strength. When I was truly ready to re-engage in my search for faith, He revealed one of the most important principles of my life. That principle stood my established and religious walk with the Master well and truly on its head.

Teresa Thevenard: Why is my heart nudging my attention? But go on.

Brian Byrne: It all happened one evening. The children were in bed and I was praying with a friend. I had asked the Lord for something I thought I needed when His words went off across the back of my brain, "It is by faith." I didn't consciously respond, but something deep inside me knew the truth of those words, so I grabbed them and truly made them my own. Then the most incredible joy exploded inside of me. It was as though all the joy I had lost during those long grey years had been bottled up and exploded in its fullest glory. I was filled up with joy as I had never been filled before. This was a totally new beginning. Even though by the next day the joy was gone, the words remained and I set out to interpret what they meant to my suddenly attentive and willing soul.

Teresa Thevenard: You've got my attention. You are saying that you engaged—re-engaged—in an active search to know how to trust Him. In all situations? Nothing left out? Does that include all your past, all your present, and all your future?

Brian Byrne: No, nothing was left out. And yes, it included all my past, present, and future. All my dreams, all my motives, and all my relationships. That sounds so simple, but I found that I was up against a very subtle opponent, for the last thing the adversary wants is for me to live by faith and be pleasing to my Father. I know he will throw everything at me to keep me stuck in a religion without power. After I began to trust Him, He began to reveal Himself in small miracles, but most of all in that astounding joy that exploded in me that night. For me joy is the measure of my trust. When I stay away from trust my joy subsides. When I let trust flourish, I am filled with that glorious joy and His Spirit sings within me to our Father. But I have found that if I let the subtleties of the world's attractions fill my vision and hold my attention then I am powerless and only a step away from wandering again in the wilderness.

Teresa Thevenard: You spoke about the world as though it was the enemy of your trust?

Brian Byrne: Certainly so. Someone told me recently that we are faced with a deteriorating world situation that naturally breeds anxiety and fear. When I look at all the news of disasters and let my attention become captured by the fragilities of world economies and the uncertainties of the world's weather, I am tempted to focus on them and not on the Lord of my trust. I believe in these days before the Lord returns things are only going to get worse. So that leaves me with two challenges for my search.

Teresa Thevenard: Two searches. I thought there was only one?

Brian Byrne: No, I believe that there are two searches. I have to fully understanding what Jesus told me that evening years ago. "It is by faith." He made me custodian of those words. Unless I go on searching for the truth behind those four words I will not be true to the trust He put in me to understand what they mean and how they apply to the life of the disciple.

Teresa Thevenard: And the second search?

Brian Byrne: There's always a negative side, Teresa. That's been fatally true in my experience. Paul listed a number of positive things that are to occupy my mind—noble, right, pure, admirable, praiseworthy things—and instructed me to "think on these things" but against each of those positive things there's a negative. And I'll be faced with all the negatives until the Lord calls me home. In my trust in Him, I will have to encounter each negative and overcome it. So I have two searches or perhaps they are parts of the same search; to learn to trust Him, and in that trust I will learn how to overcome all the obstacles to my faith.

Chapter One

Out of the Shadows

The shadows of life stole up behind me like an unwelcome visitor who was not going to announce his presence. In the beginning there was joy and then slowly like a fire turning to ash, the joy faded. The sunlight that followed that first trust had disappeared, and I was left in the dark shadows. Even serving as a teacher on an Aboriginal mission trip soon after my conversion, and then working in India did not seem to make a difference. The truth was that joy had gone, but the real tragedy was that I did not know it was missing.

There were many long years like that. Even though my life was filled with different challenges I would have called "spiritual" the joy could not be reinstated. The song that had first sung in my heart when I read the Psalms, following my conversion sitting by the side of a stream in the hills above Perth, was silent. It sang no more, like a long lost loved one who could not find a place in my heart to sing.

My wife, Marie, and I served in the Baptist church we had joined immediately after our return from India. There we lead out in worship, taught church school, and were elected for leadership positions in the church. We were probably admired as a young married couple with a commitment to the Lord and to the church. However, still the song refused to sing in my heart. There were many other voices in my spirit, all of them admirable in terms of our church culture, but the song of the Spirit of the Lord singing in worship to the Father was silent.

Discontentment about our spiritual journey filled much of our conversation at home. We asked each other, "What was missing?" We went in search of answers. I remember how Marie came home one evening after attending a meeting at a local church and reported how the minister had prayed for her. However, there was no miraculous intervention of the Holy Spirit.

The Lord was obviously following our search with His compassionate eye and knew exactly how dissatisfied we were with our form of established religion. He decided to send another person into our company. Marie happened to meet this woman first and brought her home for an evening meal. I remember her name and the fact that she was a missionary back in Australia for a brief time on furlough from Thailand. That night we talked together about faith, spirit, gifts, religion, and what the Lord had for those who would follow Him. After the meal, when the children were safely asleep we sat together on the carpet in the lounge room and prayed. There, on my knees in my living room floor, the old part of my life that was so used to shadows came to an abrupt end. Light had erupted all through my soul.

I remember asking the Lord for something special and across the back of my brain the Holy Spirit imprinted the words, "It is by faith." Looking back, I now know I had been given the key that would unlock all the doors of life and would make the mysteries of being His disciple plain to me. I did not understand then the extraordinary value of the gift I had been given; only the long and careful search into living by faith and being His disciple would make everything plain to me. Even though I could dedicate every waking hour to that search for the rest of my life, I would never be able to fathom the depths of what He had designed for me.

The morning after my prayer and after His answer I woke again to a grey world. The joy was gone but a new understanding had been born and the Lord had launched me on another part of my search to be His disciple. What was faith? How could I turn a static doctrine into an active operation? How could I release the divine energies of the Spirit into this mundane, frustrating, and confusing world of people, schedules, work, and pleasures? How could I work the divine energies into the most complex and puzzling thing of all, my relationships? I had to find out.

I do not recall when I first made the commitment to engage in the search to understand and live by faith that would radically change my life. I found the warrant for my search in the Scriptures I had come to love and revere. The Lord spoke often about faith and its place in the relationship between Himself and His people (see Matt. 8:10; Mark 5:34; Luke17:6, 22:32). Paul makes the Lord's instructions plain, "The righteous will live by faith" (Rom. 1:17; see also Gal. 3:11) and the writer to the Hebrews adds that divine dimension. If I want to please my Father and my Lord then faith is the only way into His affirmation and blessing (Heb. 11:6). Not diligent church attendance, nor submission to authority. Not even the careful study of the Scriptures or prayer. These are admirable, but not withstanding of the real relationship I desired. The primary focus in my life as His disciple had to be faith.

However, what is faith? How could I define it in such a way that I could live it, apply it, make faith operational? In human terms I cannot tell where the first insights came from, but clearly the Spirit of Truth was intimately involved in my instruction. I soon decided that faith was like a knife edge that I had to live. On one side of the knife edge was my past. I had been told by my pastor that last week's sausages are no longer any use and are best discarded. That particular image stuck in my mind. Everything I had tasted in the past, all pleasurable experiences, every achievement and success were no longer of any use. I had to walk away from them and make new beginnings every day. Paul gave words to my new understanding. "Forgetting what is behind and straining towards what is ahead, I press on towards the goal to win the prize for which God has called me heavenward in Christ Jesus" (Phil. 3:13, 14). I took Paul's example to heart and held it as the standard for my life.

If I had applied Paul's teaching only to achievements then I would have missed the point. Clearly, the past was also full of unenlightened decisions, failures, and relationships I had mismanaged. Those foolish decisions led me to the wrong side of righteousness. In all these things I had missed the mark and knew that everyone of them qualified as a sin. In fact the word "sin" can be defined as missing the mark. Sin is like an archer forever shooting arrows at a target with the arrows always falling short.

I had been taught that sin, when confessed, was forgiven. I found great comfort in the words of the Psalmist, "As far as the east is from the west, so far has He removed our transgressions from us" (Ps. 103:12). That scripture took care of my sinful past. No achievements and no sins were to be held on to. I had to let them all go and bring myself continually into the present. Again the Scriptures spoke to me, "Now is the time of God's favour, now is the day of salvation" (2 Cor. 6:2). The key word? Now! This moment! This immediate tick on the clock! But what about the future? How should I regard tomorrow?

Jesus taught His disciples many of the principles of the Kingdom of God. We all know the passage of the Sermon on the Mount (see Matt. 5–7). Towards the end of His teaching Jesus addressed the question of anxiety which is such a natural part of every Christian's experience. He concluded this passage with the words, "Do not worry about tomorrow, for tomorrow will worry about itself. Each day has enough trouble of its own" (Matt. 6:34). I decided that I could trust my Lord's instruction for He would not have given it unless He wanted it obeyed.

I teetered on my knife's edge. Nothing in the past to hold on to and nothing in the future I should grasp for. And that left only the present. Unfortunately I had missed something, but the Lord graciously permitted me to apply this simple definition of faith and did not withhold His joy. It flooded back in full measure as I learned to trust Him both with my unwanted past and with my undecided future. Trust Him unequivocally and without reservation, but what had I missed?

What I missed soon became clear to me. The present was full of decisions that had to be made and of relationships that had to be managed. There were daily choices about relationships, money, purchases, pleasures, places to go to, and things to do. There were desires that always threatened to overpower my will, and occasions where it seemed I had dug a pit of despair and buried myself.

I was learning from the Holy Spirit that I had to manage my present with the same diligence that I had learned to manage my past and future. I soon realized that the present was potentially full of so many wrong-headed decisions that would always sideline my joy. I found that out when joy refused to sing His customary love song. Joy was the measure of how effective my definition of faith was in day to day practice. However, my first operational definition of faith was defective. I needed a new one, or rather I needed to expand my learning about the operation of faith and include in my definition the present as well as the past and future.

Little by little He began to put the pieces together. I had been taught the truth of Christ living in me and found that I could represent this truth in a diagram. I took a clean page and in its center, I had drawn a circle. Within that circle I wrote my own name and the name of the Holy Trinity who lived there inside of me: the Father, the Son, and The Holy Spirit (see John 14:17, 23). That circle represented my present-time. It was the very small space I sat on and the equally tiny tick on the clock. I taught myself that within that small allotment of space and time I could depend utterly on the Ones who inhabited that place with me. However what was I to do with all the other experiences that surrounded my small circle?

Around the central circle in my diagram I drew a number of other circles. In one I wrote, "my past" and in another I wrote, "my future." In each of the other circles, I wrote words that described many of the present experiences I had to manage and cope with. Money I had to earn, my debts, repairs to our house, a car breaking down, concerns about my sons' friends, challenges at work. Each of these "cares" were individually named. The page was soon filled with circles that represented potential threats to my peace and to the joy that was His gift to me. Every circle was a potential disaster area if I failed to address each one with faith.

However, then I found another answer in my search. It felt as though the Spirit of Truth, my personal Counsellor and Teacher, was anticipating my questions. The Scriptures taught me that the Lord who lives within me has a number of significant names, and surprisingly each name as well as aspects of His character applies to each of my circles. *Jehovah*, the Lord is my strength (Isa. 12:2). *Jehovah Jireh*, the Lord will provide (Gen. 22:14). *Jehovah Shammah*, the Lord is there (Ezek. 48:35). *Jehovah Shalom,* the Lord sends peace (Judges 6:24). The Lord is my Shepherd. He will lead me (Ps. 23). He is my high tower. I always have a secure resting place (Ps. 61:3). His banner over me is love and love always stands opposed to fear (Song of Sol. 2:4; 1 John 4:18). God is light. He will expose every dark thing no matter how well I try to hide it (1 John 1:5).

As I grew in understanding of faith I found that nothing outside my central circle was outside His love, authority, grace, and forgiveness. I found that I could underwrite each circle with the words, "I trust Him in this challenge or that adversity, in that demand on my limited resources and regarding that inner emotion." As I applied these simple principles His joy would re-emerge from His hiding place and I would be filled again with all the fullness of God (see Eph. 3:19).

I found that His Love is like a garden planted with all manner of delights in which the Lord dwells. The garden is my own heart, my reborn spirit, born again by His Holy Spirit and baptized, rather immersed all over in His Spirit. There in my heart He expresses Himself daily and I feast at the table of His bounty. The Psalmist expressed this truth when he wrote, "You prepare a table before me in the presence of my enemies" (Ps. 23:5).

There are not meant to be any disfigurements in that garden of my heart. The only One who should be allowed to live in its secret precincts is He whose wisdom, grace, and love surpasses anything the world can offer. Furthermore, He and I are opposed to all that the adversary can design and inflict on my sacred inner man as he seeks to seduce me away from my joy that is my strength (see Neh. 8:10). In the garden of my heart I find consolation, authority, wisdom, and insights, but only as I trust the One who carries my heart in His hands.

Faith is the key to that relationship with Jesus. Not faith defined as some sort of mental construct, but faith that is the essence of this most personal of all relationships. It is better defined as, "trust in Jesus of Nazareth, unreserved, without conditions and involving the surrender of myself to His Lordship with all my heart and soul and mind and strength."

So I come to another beginning in my search as I set myself to understand what it means to be His disciple. In that new search also, faith in my Lord is its essential ingredient. In these pages I want to set before the reader this most personal aspect of my search; how the Lord's disciples in these years before His return are to live by faith.

Chapter Two

The Faith

Search to Understand

In my life, I have experienced comfort and I have encountered confusion. Comfort, because I know I will forever be with the One in whom I have placed my faith, the One I have trusted. Whether that is in some place called heaven, or in the New Jerusalem, or on earth during His thousand year's reign, it does not really matter. Jesus promised His disciples that He would be with them always (see Matt. 28:20).

I also encountered confusion because there are so many different ideas and definitions about what faith is. The dictionary does not take me any further in my search. If anything, it compounds my confusion. There I find faith defined as, "believing without proof," "belief in God, religion or spiritual things," "knowledge of what is believed," and "religion as in the Christian faith, the Jewish faith, the Muslim faith." Beneath these superficial and mental constructs there had to be an underlying stratum of truth informing me of the faith that I would find in the Scriptures if I searched long and hard enough for it.

In our church, subcultures faith sounds so simple. We seem to parade the term like a magic talisman we can wave before God, hoping that it stops Him in His tracks and responds immediately. We have learned to repeat Jesus' teaching like a formula for success in difficult situations when we don't know what else to do. Jesus said, "I tell you the truth, if you have faith as small as a mustard seed, you can say to this mountain, 'move from here to there,' and it will move. Nothing will be impossible for you" (Matt. 17:20). So in apparent obedience we command that this illness be gone, but it stays stubbornly in place. We pray for this one to see, but he remains blind. We ask the Lord to provide these funds, and they fail to materialize. Certainly these responses are true of so many who fill our churches. You will have heard them often when the subjects of faith and the related matter of prayer are raised. In response we say things like, "It isn't God's will," "You don't have enough faith," "We have to keep on asking and hang on to our patience," or pathetically, "The Lord knows."

I also used to respond in these same ways to the failures of what I thought was faith. However, then I began to wonder whether the problem was my faith or whether there was something more basic which I had failed in. Ever notice how uncomfortable it is to admit your own failure? Now my questions were, "Do I understand and apply faith as the Scriptures teach it in my daily walk with the Lord? Also, do I need to renew my understanding of what it means to have faith?"

As I read the Scriptures I found one Greek word that has a number of forms, though only two of those forms have compelled my search. The noun form, usually translated, "faith" or "the faith," and the verb form I prefer to translate as, "trust." In this chapter I begin with, "the faith." In the following chapters I will explore what it means to both trust, and the negative, refuse to trust.

The Faith

When Paul had completed the outward part of his first missionary journey he turned for home at Derbe and passed through the cities where he had left assemblies. In each one he spent time, "Confirming the souls of the disciples, and exhorting them to continue in the faith" (Acts 14:22, KJV). Luke used the Greek words, "the faith" here and five other times in his writings. In each case he would have known what the words meant and how they were used in the Christian world of his day. I need to let the Scriptures help me understand what the faith was for those first century disciples and from there find my own place in it.

Luke tied these words to the disciples whose faith Paul was encouraging on his homeward journey. For them, "the faith" as it is revealed in the Scriptures, is best defined as the composite of all the relationships between the five groups of participants in the faith.

Myself, a lowly sinner that has been forgiven.
The Father of Glory in relationship with myself and others called into forgiveness.
My Saviour and Lord in relationship with me as His disciple.
The Holy Spirit and His relationship with each one of us.
The relationships between the Lord's disciples.

If I focus on what the Scriptures tell me about faith I should be able to compile an image of what it means for me to be His disciple in terms of each of these relationships. However, I will have to step back from a detailed study of the Father, the Son, and the Holy Spirit. That would take me a further lifetime. Besides such understandings are best revealed progressively to each disciple by the Holy Spirit, and then expressed in the day to day order and disorder of life. I must begin with my relationship with the Father of Light who is Love.

The Father

My primary relationship is with the Father who is infinite, eternal, and who forgives those who call upon Him (Matt. 6:12; 1 John 1:5–9). Through my confession and His forgiveness I entered the relationship with the One who then acknowledged me as His son (Rom. 8:14–16). However, there is more.

The longer I live in the faith the more I am astonished by God the Father. What I find so remarkable, and that stretches my understanding to its limits and beyond, is that I truly have an intimate and immediate relationship with the One who designed all the worlds from the near side of the moon to the furthest edges of the most distant galaxies. I can call Him Father who, in His own being, is love—such love which I can never comprehend—and yet He longs to spread love's comfort and grace into my spirit from the first light of the day until the next morning's sunrise.

Throughout scripture the word "grace" appears like a constant light shining into the world's darkness. All of the writers refer to this gift that, by definition, is unmerited and doesn't depend on man's good works or is provided only because of our sinfulness. It flows to man out of the eternal heart of the Father for it is His gift to all who believe in Him. Faith is its primary requirement, for as faith flows out of the spirit of the disciple to the Father, so His grace flows back in abundant measure (see Rom. 4:16).

My friend Jenny had a long experience of church and its programmes. She was diligent in doing what was required by her church, careful to read her bible and pray, and to meet with fellow Christians. Then one morning, very early, grace came into her house. She had been reading about being His disciple and something stirred in her heart. She took heed, trusted what she was discovering about her Lord, and without any warning joy from the Father filled her heart. It was a joy she could not describe, so wonderful, like a vessel newly filled with the presence of the Father who revealed Himself to her through His own joy. That was grace she could have never earned or deserved.

The flow of His grace is never intended to be a dead end street, or a conduit with only one outlet. Jenny received His grace so that she might be its custodian to those she would meet and serve. It was His gift to her so that she might bring it as a gift to others in His kingdom. The flow must be continuous. Just as Jesus was full of grace and expressed that grace to those who would receive it (John 1:14), so also must Jenny serve His children with grace.

Paul wrote about the gifts the Father in His grace would give to His disciples. In the Greek Scriptures the words grace and gift have the same root. The first refers to the unmerited favour that is an expression of the Father's character and that flows to us from His love. The second describes the way His grace is expressed and the particular forms grace takes for the children of the kingdom (see Rom. 12:6). Paul made this clear when he described the flow of grace from the Father into His family in the form of gifts to the Body of Christ.

There are seven gifts and each one is expressed in a person. These gifts are: prophecy, service, teaching, exhorting, giving a share, taking the lead, and showing mercy. People are the gift. In each of these disciplines one or more aspects of the Father's character and will is expressed. Prophecy, so that the voice of the Father can be heard. Service, (the translation "ministry" is misleading) so that the Father can bring benefits to those being served. Teaching, so that the lives of those being taught can be shaped and formed into the image of His Son. Exhorting, so that the Father can encourage His children to continue in the faith. Giving a share, so that what the Father has provided one of His children can be multiplied into the lives of others. Taking the lead, so that the Father can guide His children in the way of faith they should take. Showing mercy, so that the Father's love can be expressed to those whose actions would rebound on them for ill.

As I seek to know the Father and to do His will He brings His peace, which is the ultimate tranquillity that surrounds and flows from the Father who Himself is the embodiment of peace (Rom. 1:7). He is never troubled by the struggles I have in this confusing world. Instead He honours me—the Father of all Glory honours this small fragile mortal—with His personal encouragement for me to endure (Rom. 15:5).

Into every day He brings me the bread I need to survive. Not simply the loaves and fishes that the multitudes feed on, but the Bread of Heaven Himself, the Father's only Son (John 6:32). In the Holy One of God I can find all the sustenance I need for my soul. I must acknowledge that being called to feed on the body and blood of the One who died and who lives again sometimes sounds like the final foolishness. God Himself affirmed this truth; however I am responsible both to understand what He meant and then to enter this most intimate of all relationships (John 6:53–58).

Therefore, I daily bring myself into that sacred place where the Father lives within me. Daily I sit at His table and worship with Him. In that place my joy rises up to Him as a song that sings to the Father who gave it.

It is to my discredit that I once lived as though this relationship only operated when I became His son and in some wrongheaded way I did not need to attend to my sonship. I possessed the doctrine that described and explained His Fatherhood and my sonship, but I was unable—or unwilling—to find a way to consciously live under the sacred covering of His care. The more I learn of Him, the more I appreciate that He purchased me to become His son when I was born into His family, and that He now sustains me in that relationship without end.

The Son

The Son is the second divinity I must understand and relate to in the faith. I met Him first when as a young man I invited Him to, "come into my heart." And He actually did. The One who responded to my first cry to Him is the One who spoke the words and the whole majestic panoply of the heavens was stretched out from infinity to infinity, with stars so distant that I could never reach them though I traveled at the speed of light for millions of years.

This eternal Being came in person into the small confined space of my own heart and washed it clean in His own blood so that it would be a fitting, resting place for His holy person (Heb. 9:14). Not only once, but daily do I need to be cleansed and made whole by the blood of the Lamb (see Rev. 7:14). I am convinced that He will continue to express Himself within my heart as long as I keep that inner sanctum free from the noise and corruption my own flesh and the world would lodge there.

In His days on earth, He became so used to the sinfulness and the waywardness of man, that I would not have surprised Him with my minor transgressions. If He could respond to the confession of the thief on the other cross and offer Him a place with Himself in paradise, He could lead me to my own confession. There are so many like the repentant thief. There are so many people in need, who need to confess their sins. He knew them all and had compassion to spare for each one. There was the Samaritan woman, who had lived with five husbands, and a sixth with whom she was now living, probably outside marriage (John 4:7–27). Matthew, the criminal tax collector (Matt. 9:9). The woman washing His feet with her tears, wiping them dry, and then kissing them and anointing them with expensive ointment (Luke 7:36–50). The crowds wandering this way and that in disarray without a shepherd (Matt. 9:36).

The sin of man, no matter how extreme and how filled with evil, was not a stranger to the Lord. He did not draw back when the Father asked Him to carry the transgressions of the whole world within Himself into the pain, shame, and degradation of crucifixion. All the evil impurities of the whole of mankind from the very beginning and including the greatest sins that man is capable, found their evil lodging place within my Lord (1 John 2:2). While dying on the cross He bore the terrible outcome of all those sins when His own Father forsook Him. Then He cried out, "My God, my God, why have you forsaken me?" (Mark 15:34).

I am confounded when I accept that the Holy One can see into the bleakest parts of my being and knows with clarity not only what I have done, but the self-centred and misdirected motives that gave birth to every one of my thoughts, words, and deeds (John 1:48, 4:29; Rev. 2:2–4). Moreover, following hard on the heels of His knowledge of me is His compassion that has never been limited. Compassion is like the air He breathes (see Mark 1:41, 6:34).

My faith in the Son of Man does not end there. Like all of those disciples who have gone before me, I accept that His knowledge of me was complete before the worlds began and that He knows me as intimately as He knows Himself. He knows the stumbles when I seek my own gratification, relationships that give nothing, but promise everything and indiscretions that leave their uncomfortable imprint on my soul.

His knowledge of me encompasses all of my present and reaches into the years left for me on earth and beyond. I like to think of Him in that not so distant future putting aside the mantle of Saviour—if that was possible—and taking on Himself the mantle of the Righteous Judge. Then everything I have kept hidden and never confessed will bear His scrutiny. The worthless rubbish I have used to build my house of faith will be burnt up. Every relationship I have wrongly constructed; every deed pursued to my advantage rather than for the benefit of another; every desire running counter to His will; every motive not constrained by His love; all will be judged.

In the terrible moment when I face Him alone on the world's stage only the precious materials that would have cost me much in faith, patience, endurance, and love will survive (1 Cor. 3:12). I will emerge from the scrutiny of His eyes, which are like a flaming fire, when I have passed through the fire of His righteous judgement. I am heartened when I remember that His judgement is also the judgement of His love (see Rev. 1:14; 1 Cor. 3:13–15).

In that moment I trust I will be able to say to Him as Paul said, "I have fought the good fight, I have finished the race, I have kept the faith. Now there is in store for me the crown of righteousness which the Lord, the Righteous Judge will award to me on that day—and not only to me but also to all who have longed for His appearing" (2 Tim. 4:7–8). Then I will be with Him forever and my part in the faith on earth will have been completed.

The Holy Spirit

The faith those first disciples encountered when they believed and were taught by Paul on his first missionary journey included their relationships with the Father and the Son. However, there was another Person with whom they had to reckon. He was unseen yet made Himself known to those first disciples in many ways. We learn the special truths about this Person not by His descriptions of Himself, for there aren't any, but because His Holy Being is embedded in so many truths in the inspired writings.

He was there in the beginning of creation when man was formed from the red dust of the earth, and it is He who preserves all things from the furthest galaxy on the distant edges of the universe to the world's microcosms of insect life (Job 33:4; Ps. 104:30). He was the agent of the Father's will when the divine seed was implanted in Mary's womb (Luke 1:35). He was the Saviour's companion, leading Him into the wilderness above the Jordan (Matt. 4:1), and it was He who was present when Jesus was tempted to worship the adversary who had promised Him all the kingdoms of the world (Matt. 4:8, 9).

Jesus told His disciples the night before His crucifixion that this Holy One, the Counsellor, the Spirit of Truth, lived with them and would be in them (John 14:16, 17). Before Pentecost He lived His life among the disciples. At Pentecost He came to live His life within each one for we read that, "All of them were filled with the Holy Spirit" (Acts 2:4).

How therefore can I make myself available to this Holy One, and what do the Scriptures teach me about the work He will do in and through me? The primary work I believe, and which is part of the faith, is to worship. Jesus told the woman at the well in Samaria, "God is spirit, and his worshippers must worship in spirit and in truth" (John 4:24). In this the Holy Spirit is my first port of call, for He is Spirit and He is also Truth (see John 15:26). I believe that I must never allow all the deceitful voices that are so often associated with the false worship of contrary idols to intrude into and compromise my worship of the Father, which is inspire by His Spirit.

If I could separate myself from these constraining earthly shackles, I would want to stand with the hosts of heaven who surround the throne; the four living creatures, the twenty four elders and the vast angelic hosts and in their company worship the Father (see Rev. 5:11–14). However, I can't do that, so I will accept the challenge of making my worship of the Father a daily, hourly, and minute-by-minute activity. The regular commitments of daily living will of course interrupt my worship, for my mind will then be otherwise engaged. Nevertheless, when I have discharged each commitment I need to immediately return to this sacred responsibility.

The Holy Spirit of the Father made Himself known to the first disciples in three different ways. He was made known in the expression of His own character within them, in the ways He manifested His presence within their hearts and minds, and in the gifts He brought to each one.

That He is a Person is without doubt for the Lord Himself refers to Him as the Comforter, the One who draws alongside the disciple (see John 14:16, 17), and who invites the disciple to walk in step with Himself (Gal. 5:25). Paul taught the disciples of the Roman assembly, "For the kingdom of God is not a matter of eating and drinking, but of righteousness, peace and joy in the Holy Spirit" (Rom. 14:17). Only a person can know righteousness, peace, and joy; never a force, an influence, or at worst a doctrine. These are attributes of the Father, the Son, the Holy Spirit, and the love of the Father. Paul wrote, "And hope does not disappoint us, because God has poured out His love into our hearts by the Holy Spirit, whom He has given us" (Rom. 5:5). The miracle of the faith is that the Spirit of the Father who lives beyond the visible universe has come into my heart.

As the Father has done and the Son has done, their lives and His own life express His own holy being.

The life of the Holy Spirit was also manifest in the disciples of the Lord in the first century. The Greek word translated "manifest" means, "to make openly known, to make visible, apparent, conspicuous." Paul taught the disciples at Corinth that it was the Holy Spirit who made Himself known to them. It was His divine life that was displayed openly and made conspicuous. Paul then went on to list different ways the Holy Spirit made His person conspicuous in the disciples at Corinth: the word of wisdom, the word of knowledge, faith, cures, operations of powers, prophecy, discerning of [the natures of] spirits, and kinds of tongues. It is important not to confuse these manifestations of the Spirit with gifts from the Father we noted before. Gifts are people engaged in the process of making the Father known. Manifestations can be one of the expressions of the life of the Spirit.

I note that my responsibility is to make myself available to receive any manifestation the Spirit brings and then to operate in them in cooperation with the Spirit Himself. If we are in any doubt about the origin of these miraculous manifestations of His life Paul goes on to assure us, "All these are the work of one and the same Spirit, and he gives them to each one, just as he determines" (1 Cor. 12:11). I ask myself, "What conditions of heart, soul, mind, and strength does the Holy Spirit look for in me before He will manifest Himself in me? I go on searching for the answer to my question and so must you.

The character of the Holy Spirit was expressed also in the different gifts He brought to the disciples in the first century. When Paul wrote to the disciples at Rome he listed a number of these gifts, which differ distinctly from the manifestations listed in his letter to the assembly at Corinth.

The Greek word translated gift, which Paul used in his letters to the assemblies at Corinth and Rome, means, "a favour, a kindness, that which is freely given, something unmerited that comes out of the Father's grace." The word also relates to the Father Himself who is the giver. It is referred to as His grace; "His kindness, His affectionate disposition towards His children, the inner beauty of His being, His gracious and courteous inclining towards those in the family of God invoking from them their thankfulness."

Peter sat in the church where I was teaching, worshipping, and listening, but he hid a part of himself that had been fractured by some encounter he had been through. Then one day one of the elders of the church came to the front and said that someone in the gathering had been fractured. Peter heard and continued to hide his pain. The elder persisted as the Spirit told him to until Peter, broken and in pain, came to the front where others gathered and prayed. The Spirit had spoken to the elder so that another of the sons of the Father could have his fracture healed.

Paul lists seven gifts in his letter to the Romans (see Rom. 12:6–8). They are: prophesy, service, teaching, exhortation, giving, ruling, and showing mercy. I note with surprise that each one of these gifts actively involves the disciple in partnership with the Father and the Holy Spirit. Although they are given because of the Father's grace and through the agency of the Holy Spirit, I am challenged to discover that the disciple must add his or her own faith to the gift. Paul includes faith only in relation to the first in the list, prophecy, but I know that faith applies to each of the remaining six (see Rom. 1:17). Little faith leads to little gift. Great faith leads to great outworking of power; but more of that later.

My Search Continues

As my search continues into the faith, my understanding is stretched to its limits as I try to comprehend a special part of the relationship the Father intends me to have with each of these eternal and infinite persons. I imagine that to them I must seem like a mere speck of dust in the vastness of the universe. This element in my relationships with each One is therefore the more astonishing. Each of these Persons not only knows all things, but has all power to pursue their purposes. They would bring me into their councils and make me part of every eternal purpose. I have to be involved if these purposes are ever to reach fruition (see Rom. 12:2; Col. 1:9).

Now my wonder is stretched to the limit, and with wonder comes awe and the inner pulse of feeling unworthy and inadequate. I struggle to see beyond the narrow walls of my limited world and to understand and play my own part in doing the divine will. All of this is packed into those two little words, "the faith."

However, there is more. Of course there is more, for God is always beyond what I have discovered. My search into the faith is always progressive; building on what is known; adding discovery and revelation to my growing understanding. So I return again to the Scriptures.

One Another

I find in the Scriptures the most satisfying and yet demanding truth, that my discipleship requires both knowledge of the mind and responses of the heart or spirit. Both! Not one or the other, and certainly never knowledge alone. James knew this when he wrote to, "the twelve tribes scattered among the nations" (James 1:1). Emerging from his letter are two strands that help us interpret the faith. The first is the inner activity of the spirit in trusting the Lord and the second is the outworking of that trust in words, deeds, and relationships.

James began his letter by affirming, "because you know that the testing of your faith develops perseverance" (James 1:3). This is the inner activity of the faith! He then directed their attention to the outworking of the faith, "In the same way, faith by itself, if it is not accompanied by action, is dead" (James 2:17). The challenge he is making to those early disciples is for them to express their inner faith in the outer action of words, deeds, and relationships.

James' first example of faith leading to action comes from Abraham the father of faith (Gen. 22:1). I imagine that this ancestor of our faith, if he was anything like me, could have rationalised the divine instruction to offer up Isaac out of existence. Perhaps he could have sent a servant with an animal sacrifice, gone himself and left Isaac at home, or disregarded the Lord's commands altogether. However, he did none of these things. James asked the question, "Was not our ancestor Abraham considered righteous for what he did when he offered his son Isaac on the altar" (see also Gal. 3:6–9 where Paul adds the inner action of faith to Abraham's outer actions of obedience). James then cited Rahab the prostitute living on the wall of Jericho, who expressed her faith in providing safe refuge for the two spies and was considered righteous for it (see James 2:21–25).

However, James is not finished with the issue. He goes on to remind his readers of the inner and outer facts of the faith with the illustration, "Suppose a brother or sister is without clothes and daily food. If one of you says to him "Go, I wish you well; keep warm and well fed" (James 2:15, 16). I believe James is adding an unwritten law of faith, "trust the Father to provide and then in obedience, be involved in that provision."

Relationships between disciples are not exempt from the outworking of the faith. James cites fights and quarrels among disciples (James 4:1), slander of one disciple by another (James 4:11), and on the positive side, the care of orphans and widows (James 1:27). These relationships should have been marked by the disciples being peace loving, submissive to one another, full of mercy, impartial in their relationships, and sincere (see James 3:17, 18).

The challenge of the faith is to receive the wisdom that comes from above and then to live out our trust in our Lord through our relationships with those whom God has called. Our understanding of this outer expression of the faith was reinforced when Paul used the term translated "brotherly love." He wrote to the disciples at Rome, "Be devoted to one another in brotherly love. Honour one another above yourselves" (Rom. 12:10). No one is exempt. No denominational bias must be allowed to separate us from one another as we live out Jesus' commandment. "A new commandment I give you: Love one another. As I have loved you, so must you love one another" (John 13:34).

When a friend like Mike comes to our house and brings his uncertainties with him I have to stop what I am doing (did I say reluctantly?), invite him in, and then patiently listen while he stumbles through the litany of his complaints. In that transaction I have to trust my Lord that He Himself will be part of the exchange with Mike who should leave our house a little lighter in his spirit, a little less uncertain, and perhaps more free to love the Father who was present in that encounter.

If I have been faithful with what the Lord has taught me and have clearly expressed those principles of faith to Mike then different parts of the faith would have come together. The Father's grace expressed in the interchange, the Son's compassion and forgiveness restoring Mike to peace and joy, and the Holy Spirit enabling this disciple to speak clearly with Mike about the principles of faith. This is faith in operation and principles of the kingdom of God at work in the place where we live.

Faith Without Power

I find all around me the uncomfortable truth that for many over the centuries, "the faith" has lost its power. Its meaning and use in contemporary language even among church people has been degraded from the high purity of truth I find in the Scriptures, to the adulterated and often meaningless fictions most dictionaries use that reflect contemporary understanding of this great word, even in our churches.

Faith certainly includes knowledge, but before we examine this word I need to lay a foundation. We start again at the beginning with the origins of knowledge and also of faith; in the garden the Lord planted in Eden.

In the very beginning the Lord planted two trees, the Tree of the Knowledge of Good and Evil and the Tree of Life (see Gen. 2:9). Both trees have counterparts in the life of faith. The first tree had one fruit, but with two characteristics, one good characteristic and one evil characteristic, the knowledge of good and knowledge of evil.

I have always known that I should turn away from knowledge of evil things whether they are images, ideas, actions or words. I should have nothing to do with anything that corrupts and defiles the creation of the Lord. True! However, I had never realised that there was only one kind of fruit on that tree. Not a good fruit and an evil fruit. Only one fruit. Now I believe that the fruit was knowledge itself. I like to think that the one fruit had two tastes, one bitter and galling—the knowledge of evil—the other sweet and palatable—the knowledge of good. Another way of looking at it is to think that eating the fruit would result in two outcomes: knowledge that could be used under the scrutiny of the Lord of Hosts, and knowledge that could become the weapon of the adversary.

When Eve and then Adam ate that fruit they opened themselves to the knowledge of both good and evil. This knowledge would embitter their lives, lead to death, and would direct them to trust in their Lord. Incidentally they opened themselves to knowledge of everything in between these two extremes as well. It is in knowledge itself that the problem of the faith lies.

I had been taught from very early in my walk with the Lord that knowledge of the Scriptures was at the heart of faith. Study the Scriptures in the original languages. Develop sound doctrine. Learn the inspired words by heart. I had been taught that the great men of God had walked this way before me and like them I could trust the knowledge of the gospel. All good! All praiseworthy! All commendable! I have done them all, but in some surprising way my search for good knowledge somehow missed the mark.

Jesus told His disciples before He died, "I am the way and the truth and the life" (John 14:6). The danger is that I will separate knowledge of the truth from the person who is the truth. I find myself faced with the trap of taking the truth, making it into a golden bird, locking it in a golden cage, and throwing away the key. Or perhaps putting the key in my own pocket and restricting its use to anyone not approved by my version of the truth.

The same danger is expressed when I use my knowledge of a windstorm to write a treatise on the wind as though required by a critical examining body. Such a document, however many truthful facts it contained, could never expose me to the gentleness of the wind in my face or the fury of the hurricane that I must take refuge from. I would forever be safe because I would have taken refuge in knowledge of the wind without exposing myself to its remorseless truth and power.

I touch the same principle in my relationship with my Lord. I can write about Him all my life and never be touched by His love. I can retreat into my knowledge of doctrine about sin and forgiveness and never stand before Him humbled to confess the transgressions that have plagued me. I can recite the most meaningful prayers with the most intense emotions and greatest ardour and never know the grace that flows from His throne. I could know next to nothing about the Spirit, about repentance, about forgiveness, or about faith. Not as they have to work themselves out in my life.

What do I conclude? Knowledge describing truth is good and profitable, but only as it informs my discipleship and leads me into the arms of my Lord where I am sheltered from the destructive forces that the knowledge of evil can visit on the disciple. Knowledge without those inner responses that the Lord asks of us has no power.

The disciples discovered that principle when they were confronted by the demon possessed son on the plains below Mount of Transfiguration (see Mark 9:18). Although they had seen the Lord cast out demons, and had themselves been involved in that service, they could not deal with the demon possessed boy and his distressed father. They had the knowledge, but the power was missing. We in the twenty first century urgently need to attend to this problem in our understanding of the faith.

Knowledge of the Lord is a secure place for my mind, but my response to Him, although it involves my mind and what I know, has to come from a heart that has experienced the full blown glory of His forgiveness and love.

When I am at rest in that secure place—loving Him and being loved—I am able to deny the insidious attractions of wrong, or partial knowledge and the temptation to focus only on the compelling voices of knowledge of that which is good.

I should be focusing on better knowledge. However, if I go no further than what the mind can know and leave my spirit idle, I would be lowering Him to the sidelines of my life and be locked into isolation from the Lord. With my heart facing Him and with my life in His hands I can drink deeply of the eternal life that is His life within me, which the tree of life prefigured so long ago. The faith with the power of His life and presence, once lived by the saints in the first century, is waiting to be resurrected in this age before He returns.

Chapter Three

Who Is He?

Who Is He?

When I asked the Lord to come into my heart I had little idea who He was. I had not read the Scriptures nor had I the benefit of teaching from Godly men. I came to that moment aware only that I must reach out to Him. I understand now that the Lord of glory never lets my ignorance be an obstacle to His call. When He is responding to the cry of a human heart He overlooks any conceptions or misconceptions we might have and responds in His grace to our heart's cries.

Sometime after my conversion I wrote a poem that expressed my search to know who He is.

> Who is He who sits upon the mountains
> And rides the whirlwind and the hurricane?
>
> Who is He who wrought the tapestry
> Of stars along the purple universe?
>
> Who is He who paints the daffodil
> With gold and gilds the butterfly?
>
> Who is He who gave His Son to suffer
> Insult, agony and death?
>
> Is He God who did these things that I
> May curse my Saviour to His face and die?
>
> Or does He have some better thing for me?
> Of broken fetters and eternity?

There has not been a time when a new understanding has completed my knowledge of Him or led me to a kind of spiritual plateau where I could at last give up the search. Instead the search to know who He is has always been there. Sometimes consciously and at other times it has been the Holy Spirit's own agenda as He leads me further into truth. However, sometimes I have slid back into a vague kind of grey unknowing when it seemed I didn't care whether I knew Him or not.

For a long time my concept of the Lord was dysfunctional because it did not allow me to take a step forward in my trust. Like me, there are those today who cannot or will not come to the Father. Regrettable past—and even present—experiences of their own fathers have turned them inward and away from the truth. In not knowing who they can trust they fall away from the secure place that trust generates and take refuge in all kinds of inner doubts and fears. Such people have turned their rebellion against their human father into a desperate rejection of the eternal Father whose love ever reaches out, only to encounter the unyielding barricades of their unbelief.

We have all encountered such people, who with little understanding of who they can trust remain locked into this place of unknowing. Their spiritual lives become like the stagnant waters of a pool with no streams flowing in to alleviate the morass of anger, rebellion, and fear they have become so accustomed to. They are held prisoners to the ignorance from which Jesus came to set them free.

It has become important in my discipleship for me to continue this search to know the One in whom my trust has to reside. He has made His eternal commitment to live within the confines of my own heart (see Gal. 2:20) and therefore calls me to match His commitment with my own. I need to learn how to trust Him and then how to live, so that His life and personality can be expressed in my own life.

I have never been alone in this challenge. Some of the men and women He encountered on His journeys across the Holy Land had the same problem. His own family had reached the conclusion that He was out of His mind (Mark 3:19–21). The teachers of the law, unable to fit Him into their religious scheme of things, attributed His powers to Beelzebub (Mark 3:22). Neither His family nor the leaders of the Jews could receive any benefits from the Lord because their understanding of Him locked them into unbelief.

However, the centurion who came to the Lord asking for help with his suffering and paralysed servant knew who Jesus was. When the Lord told the centurion he would come immediately to his house, the man replied, "Just say the word and my servant will be healed. For I [like you] am a man under authority." His understanding of who the Lord was set his faith free. Jesus acknowledged this when He said; "I have not found anyone in Israel with such great faith" (see Matt. 8:5–10).

Like His family, the Jews, and the centurion, our concept of the One we trust influences how we may respond to Him. If those whom the Lord faced in that century could speak, they would have something to tell us about the One who faced them with their own truth and lead them out of their personal darkness into the light of the Son of God. Some may have to testify how they had been trapped in their own darkness and how their encounter with the Lord had been like a judgement because of their inability to trust Him.

This was so for the two men bound to their own personal crosses on each side of Jesus. Both had a view of the One dying between them and out of that view flowed their motives, words, and actions. It was like a fountain that owed its origin to something found deep in the soul of man. Out of one man, bitterness. Out of the other, repentance. Both of these men had to ask and answer the question, Who is He? They then had to be bound into their answer like a man either trapped as in a stairwell or walking free in a garden of delights.

The one lived in darkness because of his blindness, but chose to reach out to the light. The other chose blindness as a way of life and lived in darkness. Jesus saw them both and undoubtedly loved them both. The one He led from darkness into light; the other the Lord had no choice but to confirm in his darkness.

There were two other men Jesus encountered who were accustomed to darkness. The first was a beggar born blind. The second was a Pharisee who thought he could see, but actually remained locked in the darkness he thought was light.

The Man Born Blind

The account of the man born blind is reported by only one of the gospel writers. It was John who examines the events of that Sabbath at the Temple in careful detail. In his record John weaves together two strands of our faith, who Jesus was to the blind man, and what it means to believe.

The blind man's family was undoubtedly very poor. The blind child delivered into his mother's arms had grown into a man that could not be supported by his parents. In their penurious desperation they would have daily brought him to the entrance of the Temple or its sacred precincts, spread his mat where he would sit and beg, and helped him to find a comfortable place. We don't know his name nor do we know how old he was when he was first brought to the temple to beg. However, I can imagine the Lord pausing as He passed that way and looking at the blind man.

The disciples wanted to know who had sinned, the blind man or his parents, for it was widely believed that sickness and even death were God's punishments for such disabilities. Jesus corrected their ignorance with three statements about His own person. The first truth: "this has happened so that the work [literally "energies"] of God might be displayed in his life." The second truth: "As long as it is day we must do the work of Him who sent me. Night is coming when no one can work." Then the third truth, "While I am in the world, I am the light of the world" (John 9:3–5).

Now here in this small corner of the world Jesus encountered darkness, both behind the blind eyes of this beggar, and in the understanding of the Jews who would take issue with the Lord's mercy. Standing beside the blind man He spat on the ground, made a small swatch of mud, and bending down pasted the mud on the unseeing eyes.

Nothing is said about the blind man's response to this surprising happening. Perhaps it was astonishment? Most certainly, for no one would have ever treated him as this stranger had done. Who the Stranger was and where He had come from was unknown to him, but then he heard the surprising words, "Go, wash in the Pool of Siloam." John then reports, "So the man went and washed, and came home seeing" (John 9:7).

This passage in the record leaves out a great deal. The man would not have been able to go to the Pool of Siloam on his own. He was blind. We are not told how he found his way to the pool with the mud still plastered on his unseeing eyes. There are no details of his delight and wonder at being able to see things he had only heard about. Nor would he have been able to return home for he had never seen what home looked like or where it was located. Others would have had to take his hand and lead him on the first part of his journey into wholeness, to the Pool where he washed his face, and then home. The involvement of others in this first part of his journey into faith is like a parable that can tell us a great deal about similar journeys of so many in our own age.

When he got home he encountered his neighbours who could not believe it was the same man. Their comments are faithfully recorded by John, adding to the record and emphasizing the power of what had taken place (see John 9:7–11). They wanted to know where the One who had healed him was, but the healed man couldn't tell them. He didn't know. John tells us that the man did know something, and that was the basis of all that followed. He knew His name. Jesus!

There is little point in exploring all the details of this carefully recorded encounter. It is sufficient here to focus on the relationship between Jesus and the man suddenly dwelling in the light. For something was beginning to form in the man's mind and heart, like a seed planted and ready to spring into life.

John tells us that at first the man knew only Jesus' name. Then after questioning, which failed to deter him, he was able to recount carefully for the second time what had happened. Then perhaps in exasperation at the Pharisee's question he responded with the rather terse statement, "He is a prophet" (John 9:17). His understanding of who had healed him had taken another step into faith. However, there was more.

The Pharisees in their blindness would not let the issue go. First they sent for his parents and questioned them, though they failed to get any satisfaction. Then they called again for the man and had him repeat what had taken place. He replied to them, "I have told you already and you did not listen. Why do you want to hear it again? Do you want to become His disciples, too?" (John 9:27). As though he was affirming his own tentative steps into become Jesus' disciple.

The man's last question tells its own story. It is as though, in the time between feeling the mud on his eyes and facing the blindness of the Pharisees, the man was being brought by the Holy Spirit—by whom else—to the beginnings of belief. This is born from the man's final response to the Pharisees, "Nobody has ever heard of opening the eyes of a man born blind. If this man were not from God he could do nothing" (John 9:32, 33). In other words, Jesus had to have come from God.

They threw him out of the Temple. This was the most extreme banishment that the leaders of the Jews could inflict on one of their own race. If it passed through all the stages of excommunication the man would be treated as a leper, would be required to sit on the ground, and allow his hair to grow wild. Bathing and anointing himself would be forbidden and people would be unable to walk closer to him than four cubits (A cubit was equivalent to six handbreadths, about 1.4 metres. Four cubits would have been between five and six metres.). If he died he would not be permitted a normal funeral; no one would be allowed to mourn him, and stones would be thrown on his coffin. The man born blind and now healed was thrown out of the temple. This was like becoming a dead man.

Time must have passed and Jesus and His disciples would have moved on, but John tells us that Jesus looked for the man and when He found him the Lord took his newly becoming disciple the last step into belief. He asked him, "Do you believe in the Son of Man" (John 9:35). John records the man's response. "Who is He sir?" the man asked. "Tell me so that I may believe in Him." We have to examine the Lord's conversation with the once blind man in careful detail for it has much to teach us about faith. However, first we have to turn our attention to a man born with his sight intact, but who was blind.

The Pharisee

He is not named and he exists only in the record as part of a group. I have chosen to isolate this one man as their spokesman so that I can highlight in sharp relief the difference between this religious person and the man once blind who could now see. This Pharisee had to contend with his own concept of who Jesus was, but more of that later.

Pharisees did not exist prior to the exile. They possibly came into being in part as a reaction to the unpredictable reign of Antiochus Epiphanes. At that time, around 167 BC, a group of Jews known as the Hasidim, were troubled with the increasing move of the Jews towards Greek values and customs. Instead they sought to emphasize loyalty to Yahweh and the covenant relationship with their God. The Pharisees grew out of the Hasidim and inherited their conservative loyalty to the law. Over the years since their inception the Pharisees had worked diligently to build a hedge around the Torah—the five books of Moses—that they acknowledged was the sacred core of their faith. In this they believed they were accountable to God to protect the common people from error and in that they could not be faulted.

It would be a serious error to think that we should judge all Pharisees in the stern words of our Lord, whose words were directed towards their understanding of the kingdom of God, and towards the way they had, "shut the kingdom of heaven in men's faces" (Matt. 23:13).

The individual Pharisee we will study was once a child exposed to all the much loved rituals of his family's faith, repeated their prayers, and was taught to ask the questions at Passover that would prompt his father to expound their secular and religious history from Abraham to their present time.

Up to the age of six he would have been taught first by his mother and then by his father all the stories of their faith, all the prayers and benedictions, and all the traditions and feasts through which their faith was expressed. On leaving the house as a child, he would, like his father, have reached out to touch the Mesusah, the shiny metal case attached to one of the door posts that contained two passages of scripture, kissed the finger that had made contact with that sacred object, and then uttered a prayer of benediction.

At the age of six he would have been enrolled in the school attached to the synagogue and there begun his professional education, first in Leviticus and in reading and writing Hebrew. From there he would have gone on to the secondary school where his education would have extended to the other four books of the Torah and to the histories, the psalms, and the prophets. He would have gone with his parents to the Temple and witnessed in awe the sacrifices and the chants of the priests reciting the psalms while the drink offering was poured out. For this growing up and soon to be Pharisee the knowledge of God was everything. The sole object of his education was to prepare him in all its carefully worded detail for service of God in every aspect of his daily life.

From the schools in the synagogue he would have continued in his training in the other sacred books. Not only the Scriptures, but the Mishnah and the Talmud that he learned to value even more than the five books of Moses. The Mishnah was a record of conversations of the Rabbis. In it they discussed the interpretation of each part of the five books of Moses. It was in this teaching that our future Pharisee would have learned his binding legal obligations and the way he had to present himself in public. There were chapters in the Mishnah that dealt with everything from the corners of fields, the sale and storage of fruits, the disposal of leaven, the seating of money changers in the Temple, casting lots, the throwing of objects, prayers for rain, sacrilegious objects, methods of purification, permitted dress for the Pharisee, and stalks of fruit that conveyed impurity. The list goes on and on. Nothing was left out.

From the Mishnah he would have moved on to the Talmud which he believed was the oral law delivered by God to Moses, parallel to but separate from the first five books of the Bible. In the study of these two bodies of literature as well as the Torah, our future Pharisee would have been taught the legal obligations that would effectively bind him into all the rituals and obligations that would separate him from the great mass of the unwashed, the uneducated, and the sinners. He came to believe that because they did not know the law they were effectively under a curse.

The Pharisee's education, for all its gentle beginnings in the arms of his mother and sitting at the feet of his father, put a barricade between his understanding of the law in all its ramifications, and Jesus' teachings about the kingdom of God. Our Pharisee would have had little comprehension that there was any difference between his religion and God's kingdom on earth; and therein lay his blindness.

This was the man now confronted by the blind man now seeing. It had been the Sabbath and that was part of the problem. Our Pharisee knew that three actions of the Lord were forbidden by law for the Sabbath: making clay, applying a remedy for an ailment such as blindness, and the application of saliva to the eye. Our Pharisee was locked into his understanding and could not "see" the delight of the man now seeing or the wonder of his friends and neighbours as they brought the former beggar to them.

The Pharisee expressed who he believed Jesus was in three ways. In the first place he declared that, "This man is not from God for he does not keep the Sabbath" (John 9:16). In the second place, after speaking with the healed man, he declared, "We know this man is a sinner" (John 9:24). Then in the third place we find our representative Pharisee saying, "We know that God spoke to Moses, but as for this fellow, we don't even know where he comes from" (John 9:29).

In our Pharisee we find a man securely locked into the prison cage his religion had fastened about him. His image of Jesus dictated how he should respond to the Lord. He was not from God. He was a sinner and a fellow who comes from nowhere. How could the Pharisee trust Him? What else could he do but retreat into the darkness behind his barricade of religious edict and regulation?

After the Lord had found the man born blind he delivered his final damning verdict to the Pharisee. "For judgement I have come into the world, so that the blind will see and those who see will become blind" (John 9:39). Our Pharisee who we imagine was in the group of those listening to Jesus, asked the question, "What? Are we blind too," And Jesus replied, "If you were blind you would not be guilty of sin; but now that you claim you can see, your guilt remains" (John 9:40, 41). The Pharisee would indeed have affirmed he could see, but it was only the sight that fastens attention on the minutiae of the law, religious obligation and tradition, and not the sight that sees the Lord who is the pathway into faith.

Have you ever encountered Christian people who listen politely to your testimony of the Lord's grace but their eyes give them away? They are listening, but they don't seem to hear. Your words take them only so far and then they encounter their own blindness and draw back.

Are there Pharisees in the church today? Not in name, but many will fall back or retreat into religious obligation and use doctrine as a barricade behind which they can hide from the eyes of the Lord. This is the story of the countless denominations around the world today. For only He will search out and reveal the thoughts and intents of the heart (see Heb. 4:12).

Lord, I Believe

The Lord knew that his dealings with the man born blind were not complete. One thing more remained. John tells us that Jesus found out that the Pharisees had thrown him out of the synagogue and engaged him in the final steps of becoming one of His disciples. He asked him the question, "Do you believe in the Son of Man?" (John 9:35). To the unthinking reader Jesus' question may seem rather ordinary, but contained in the Greek verb, "believe in" is a world of meaning that often passes the casual reader by. However, before we examine what Jesus really said we need a little Greek grammar.

In the Greek there are three constructions for the verb believe. The first is *pisteuo en*, which means "believe on," and refers to our trust in the One who is the foundation of our trust. The second is *pisteuo epi,* best translated as "believe upon." It is trust that brings the one who trusts into rest from the works that would consume him and divide his attention from the Lord. The third construction, the one that Jesus used with the man once blind is *pisteo eis*, which means "believe into" and it is this verb that brings us to the threshold of our discipleship.

The preposition "into" which accompanies the verb carries with it the idea of movement into the interior of a place such as a house or a room. In this case it is movement of the one who trusts into the centre of the Son of Man, or literally into the heart of Jesus. It is trust without conditions. Trust that has no reservations. It is trust that brings with it the surrender of the disciple to the Lord.

The man born blind asked the Lord, "Who is he, sir? ... Tell me so that I may believe in him" (John 9:36). The man understood who Jesus was and what He was saying, for he used the same Greek words the Lord used. He had taken the next step into becoming His disciple, acknowledging the claims the Lord would have on his life and the inner response the Lord required of him.

The Lord reached back into the heart of this man who had come out of one darkness and was about to venture out of a second. "You have now seen him; in fact, he is the one speaking with you" (John 9:37). Such a gentle reminder of the state out of which the Lord had delivered him; for once he had been unable to see in the literal sense, but also in the spiritual sense. He had been delivered from his first blindness and now would be delivered from the second. "Then the man said, 'Lord, I believe,' and he worshiped him" (John 9:38).

Like the man born blind I came also to the end of one part of my search and to the beginning of another. I was blind for my heart could not see the One who had called me so patiently. For so many years I, like the lamentable Pharisee, relied on the constructs of my doctrine without faith, trying to mix my sight with the blindness that Satan, the adversary, would keep me ensnared within. However, when faith truly came, when my trust in Him as the foundation of my faith entered its fullest expression, I found rest as I unconditionally and without reservation surrendered all of my being to His Lordship. I found my own place in His heart and He came to live in mine. In those transactions my faith was complete.

I take comfort in the fact that Jesus sees all the darkness in my life and is not deterred. Nor does He take refuge, as the Pharisees did, in religious justification. He knows me with all my blindness. As the Light of the World He continues to reveal to me those things that I have hidden away in my personal inner darkness. Who do I trust? The One who sees me as I really am and who doesn't draw back.

Chapter Four

Believing Into the Word of God

The Questions

The further I walk with the Lord the more I find how deep, wide, long, and high are the truths that surround me, and the less I can claim to know how they apply to my own discipleship. This applies to my faith, or more specifically to what it means to trust Him. I have questions such as: How is trust born? What sustains my trust in the midst of so many situations that threaten to destroy it? Also, what is the relationship between my trust in Him and the words He speaks into my soul?

Very early in my Christian life I was taught that all the answers to such questions were in the Scriptures and that I had to seek them in the word of God. Clearly I had to know how to read this amazing volume of books, but the more I read the Scriptures and the more I opened my mind to understand what they were saying, the more I encountered odd patches of puzzlement. This was particularly so with the term, "the Word of God."

Two of the references that puzzled me were Luke's statements in Acts. He wrote that, "the word of God grew and multiplied" (Acts 12:24, KJV). I asked myself; How could the Scriptures grow and multiply? However, there was more to add to my puzzlement. Luke also wrote, "all they which dwelt in Asia heard the word of the Lord," (Acts 19:10, KJV). I knew that both these records referred to activities of the disciples during a period when the New Testament scriptures had not yet been written, and when the Old Testament scriptures were safely located in synagogues. There had to be a way to account for these puzzling texts. Did the term, "the Word of God" actually refer to the Scriptures or did I have to rethink my Biblical doctrines?

I realised that such a search would take me along the borderline between acceptable doctrine and heresy. Still I had to persist for I believed that the entire Scriptures were inspired and held together like the most delicately worked silver filigree. I had been taught that each word or phrase had to be read in the context of the sentence in which it was found in, in the paragraph, in the book, and in both the Testaments. I knew if I looked hard and carefully enough the Scriptures themselves would resolve my puzzlement.

The first discovery in my search to understand was that there was not one Greek word translated, "word," but two; *logos* and *rhema*. Then the next discovery shocked me and showed me how far from the truth I really was. It was the definitions of the words *logos* and *rhema*.

> *Logos*: the spoken word connected with and expressing the inward thought and being of the One who spoke it. Not the written word about Him. *Logos* referred to the entire spoken words of Jesus that expressed who He was, in the same way that He Himself in all His being expressed who the Father was. Spoken words meant that people were listening for and understanding what Jesus was saying to them. Not what they were reading about Him.

> *Rhema*: what is spoken; a sentence, saying, speech, discourse, declaration, command or promise; a word as part of a sentence; a sentence as part of a discourse; a portion as part of the whole; a *rhema* as part of the *logos*.

These definitions led me back to the One who heard from the Father and then spoke those words into the hearts and minds of His disciples (see John 14:24). We know Him as Jesus of Nazareth. It is easy to reason that Jesus spoke the words that were written down under the inspiration of the Holy Spirit and recorded in the Scriptures and that are therefore the word of God. Sounds reasonable, but I needed more.

My next two discoveries faced me with a terrible and disconcerting truth. They took me beyond the written and spoken word, and I found myself face to face with a person, to the Word of God Himself. The first reference says, "In the beginning was the Word, and the Word was with God, and the Word was God. He was with God in the beginning. Through him all things were made; and without him nothing was made that has been made" (John 1:1–3). The second is a record of what the prophet saw with heaven standing open at the end of time. There he saw "a white horse, whose rider is called Faithful and True. With justice he judges and makes war. His eyes are like blazing fire, and on his head are many crowns. He has a name written on him that no one knows but he himself. He is dressed in a robe dipped in blood, and his name is the Word of God" (Rev. 19:11–13).

From the beginning to the end. In the beginning the Word of God was the Creator of all things. At the end the Word of God will be the Judge of all men. He is the One who died and defied the claims of death and hell, and is now seated at the right hand of His Father and my Father (see Heb. 1:3). How can I stand before this

One who holds infinity and eternity as well as my life in His hands? The One whose eyes are a blazing fire. If I came face to face with the majesty of the Word of God I would be compelled to fall prostrate at His feet and to cover my eyes.

Someone once wrote that my God was too small. What I believe he meant was that we had relegated the eternal Lord of Glory, the Creator of all things, ruler over the vast expanses of the heavens, and Master of the angelic beings of that infinite world, the Word of God Himself, to a little world we call church. Here in church we refer to Him with prosaic sayings, jargon, and clichés that are like the rhinestones on a garment. They are like objects that have no depth and no substance except that we like them to sparkle. I believe that I, and so many others, have become satisfied with the imitation when the pearl without price was within our reach and we didn't know it. We express our faith in small expectations that reach no further than the ceiling, being content with the crumbs under the Master's table rather than being able to feast with the Word of God Himself (see Rev. 3:20).

He Himself is the *Logos*, and I am ashamed. However, I have to go further in my search to understand if I am to read the Scriptures correctly and apply their truths to my own discipleship. First I have to hear what the Scriptures tell me about themselves. What are they? How did we get them? What use are they to me in this walk as His disciple? They themselves tell me the answers.

Jesus, Paul, James, and Peter referred to the collection of Old Testament scriptures as that which is written, or, "the holy writings" (see Matt. 21:42 and Rom. 1:2). Included in the writings were the writings that came to man through Moses simply called, "the law," and the writings that came through His prophets, known in Jewish circles as, "the prophets" (Rom. 16:26).

When Paul wrote to Timothy he spoke of "the writings" that refer, not to a collection of books as in the Old Testament, but to different separate writings, such as his own letters and the gospel of Mark. He then wrote, "every writing is God breathed and profitable for teaching, for reproof, for correction, for instruction in righteousness in order that the man of God may be fitted [having been] furnished for every good work" (2 Tim. 3:16, 17, literal translation in Greek).

Centuries after he wrote to Timothy these inspired writings were canonised and became known as the New Testament, which when printed with the Old Testament became our Bible. It lies open before me as I write, for out of these inspired documents will come the principles that teach me how to live this present life and trust Him as His disciple.

When I read its inspired pages I listen for the One who speaks into my heart. Sometimes He uses the Scriptures to speak to me, but He is not bound to speak in this manner. Whether He uses the Scriptures or not, His *rhema* will bring light, healing, and release from captivity and the revelation of truth if I heed and act on what He is telling me. In His *rhema* I will also discover direction for my day-by-day walk with Him. Like those first disciples I must always be attentive to the voice of the Word of God, lest I miss something that will add to His will being done on earth as it is done in heaven.

Faith Comes by Hearing

Paul wrote words that are at the heart of the life of faith. The words in the Greek text are cryptic, "Then the faith [is] from hearing and the hearing through a word of Christ" (Rom. 10:17, literal translation in Greek). Paul is telling me that my trust in Him is brought into being through a *"rhema* of Christ," a particular word spoken into my heart by the Lord Himself. I hear His word, and I stand in awe of the One who would take the time to speak with one of the least of His saints. I know that what He has spoken into my heart is a mirror of the will He wants accomplished. My trust in my Lord is not self-sufficient for it must always be accompanied by obedience to what He has spoken into my heart. Sometime for my own instruction, and sometimes for the spiritual welfare of another.

Anna was ill and in the hospital. She lived next door to us. Her children played with our sons, but she had not yet found faith. We decided to visit her so that a friend who knew the Spirit's voice could visit her in the hospital. Anna was most gracious and listened to all that we said, but without response. My friend and I both knew our words hadn't penetrated deep enough to kindle faith, so we left her in her lonely hospital room and went home.

I wasn't satisfied with our visit. We had left Anna in her darkness and I was determined to visit her again. This time I asked the Lord what to say and He imprinted two words in my spirit; "repentance and faith." When I arrived Anna was sitting near the window. After our greetings I asked her if the words "repentance and faith" meant anything to her. Her response was immediate. Tears welled up. I laid hands gently on her, prayed for her and returned to my seat. When the tears stopped she looked at me in amazement, "What is happening to me?" she asked, and then explained, "I feel all filled up." Joy had come into her suddenly renewed spirit in response to the words the Lord had given me before I left home. He knew that His words would bring life to Anna, but only if I used my inner ear to listen to what He was saying and instruct my will to obey His instructions.

My trust is not a conjured up thing. It is not something I can make happen. It doesn't depend on how much or how well I know what faith is. The Scriptures teach me that my trust in Him only comes about when He speaks into my inner ear, I have accepted that word, and it has born the fruit of trust that it was intended for. In this sense my mind plays only a limited part in this transaction, for it is into my heart or spirit that He speaks this word, this *"rhema,"* and it is from my spirit that my trust in Him comes daily to birth (see Rom. 10:10).

When Jesus told His disciple, "blessed are your eyes because they see, and your ears because they hear" (Matt. 13:16), He wasn't talking about the physical organs of sight and hearing, but about their reception of His words that came to them from the Father. I know that I have within my spirit, unseen and unbidden, the capacity to see what the Spirit shows me and to hear what the Lord is saying. It is these active spiritual facilities of sight and hearing that the Lord needs in order to communicate His *rhema* to His disciples.

The Parable of the Sower

Part of my understanding of trust in my Lord has its counterpart in the parable of the sower (see Matt. 13:1–23). Jesus included in that parable a number of principles about hearing the Word of the Lord that I believe are intended to shock me out of my complacency as a "make believe" Christian.

In that parable Jesus revealed four conditions in the human spirit that I must understand if I am to listen for and obey the Word of the Lord. The first is lack of understanding or my unwillingness to understand. It is like the atheist who wants to argue, or the part time Christian who won't focus on what the Lord is saying to him. I compare this to the seed that fell on the path as the adversary snatched it away from my understanding.

The second is the lack of depth in my understanding, being content with the superficial interpretation; the pretty rhinestones that are only ornaments on the garment and not the real garment. Such lack of depth means that I receive the Lord's word to me with joy, but when I encounter difficulties that bring pain, confusion, frustration, fear, doubt or so many other emotions, I will allow those voices to distract me from what I hear from the Lord.

The third refers to the worries of this life and the deceitfulness of wealth, the seed that was choked and had to compete with the noises of my flesh and from the world. We tend to think that anxieties are inevitable, but when we accept anxiety we allow it run counter to our trust in the One we follow. The Lord devoted a significant portion of His Sermon on the Mount to this subject (see Matt. 6:25–34). Certainly His words, "the deceitfulness of riches" speak loudly in my own ears and echo the hollowness of the supposed good things that riches are supposed to buy, and which we see advertised so beguilingly all around us.

The final part of the Lord's parable is about the one who hears the word spoken in his heart and understands what he is hearing. The Greek word Jesus used for understand is *sunieis*. This word carries a weight of meaning far beyond mental comprehension of the meaning of words. It means, "to bring together the different part of a message into a whole; to collect, apprehend, grasp, comprehend, understand, lay to heart and be earnestly occupied with what is being revealed."

Such understanding does not refer to a passing interest in what is being heard, like a Christian attending a church who affirms that the pastor's sermon was excellent, or like the man who looks in a mirror and takes no note of what he has seen (see James 1:23–25). Instead understanding refers to a commitment to understand and to act.

This depth of understanding finds an echo in the words of Luke about the first disciples after Pentecost. "They devoted themselves to the apostles' teaching and to the fellowship, to the breaking of bread and to prayer" (Acts 2:42). The words "devoted themselves" are translated from *proskartereo*, which means, "to be strong or firm towards any person or thing, to endure, to persevere, to be continually in or with that person or thing." In the case of the first disciples, they continually devoted themselves to understand and live as disciples of the Lord in fellowship with the One who is the Word of God.

The words of the parable relating to the good seed falling on good ground challenge me. I am embarrassed to think how often I have been content with superficial understanding, and have not taken the time and effort to fit all the parts of the mosaic of truth I am hearing from the Lord into a single frame of reference for my life. There was a woman like that who had to face similar challenges before she came to trust the One who spoke with her. She was the Samaritan woman the Lord encountered at Jacob's Well in Sychar. In His conversation with the woman I find that Paul's words about faith coming by hearing and hearing through a Word of Christ were literally applied by the Lord to the life of this sinful woman.

The Woman at the Well

Jesus and His disciples had for some time been in the north east of Judea though the exact location is not known. He had been teaching and His disciples had been baptising. From there it would have been a difficult day's journey along back country tracks until they came to the north south road from Jerusalem where they would have then turned north towards the ancient site of Shechem. I wonder as they drew near to Shechem, if Jesus and His disciples talked about this place where Jacob had been buried after his body had been brought up from Egypt. It was at Shechem that Joshua called an assembly of the Israelites and set up a great stone under the oak tree as a testimony to the covenant made that day between Israel and the Lord.

The history of Samaria in which Shechem is located is difficult, convoluted, and records are scarce. From Assyrian records we know that Sargon II besieged and captured the city of Samaria in 721 BC and deported 27,290 persons of Hebrew origin. They were replaced with men and women from regions under Sargon's control with different religions and languages (see 2 Kings 17:24–40). Samaria then became a racial mix as the purity of the Hebrew blood was diluted and their faith corrupted.

We know however that none of the pagan gods brought by these mixed races to Samaria or their customs survived. Samaria remained essentially Hebrew. However, traditional Jews would have nothing to do with Samaritans and certainly not with a Samaritan woman. Whether this was because of the Samaritan's mixed race or because they had developed a bastard kind of Hebrew religion, we cannot tell.

As the Lord and His disciples drew near Shechem the day would have been drawing to a close, and they would have been hot, tired, and hungry. According to Roman time it was approaching 6 p.m. (See John 4:6. The sixth hour according to Roman time was 6 p.m. According to Hebrew time keeping it was noon. I believe that it was evening when the woman came to the well and not during the heat of midday.)

This was the heart of Samaritan country for atop Mount Gerizim rising steeply to their left in the fading sunlight were the ruins of the Samaritan temple that had been destroyed more than a hundred years before the Lord passed that way.

There are no records telling us when the temple on Mount Gerizim was built, but one legend has it that it had been constructed by a Samaritan named Sanballat, one of the three men who opposed Nehemiah as he supervised the rebuilding of the wall of Jerusalem (see Neh. 2:19). Nehemiah records that a priest had married Sanballat's daughter contrary to God's rule that the priestly line was not to be corrupted by intermarriage (see Lev. 21:6–8, 14, 15). Nehemiah ordered that the marriage be brought to an end and that the man leave the priesthood. According to the legend Sanballat built the rival temple on Mount Gerizim and there installed his son-in-law as priest in defiance of Nehemiah whom he hated, and in opposition to the Hebrew priesthood that served the temple in Jerusalem (see Neh. 4;13, 28, 29).

Just beyond Shechem was the small town of Sychar lodged in the valley between Mount Gerizim to the south and Mount Ebal to the north. It was there that Jacob had dug the well that bears his name, going down deep through the limestone and tapping into the springs that abound in that region (today it is partially filled with rubbish and stones and has the ruins of a church that had been built over it). When Jesus came to the well it was filled with abundant water and He sat on the stone parapet around the well while His disciples went into the village to buy food. John, who is the only one who records these events, probably stayed with the Master.

The Samaritan woman came to Jacob's well to draw water. That was the apparent reason. The deeper reason for her visit involved the One who would be there that day and who would look into the woman's heart and speak of things that would bring her to faith. A chance encounter? I don't think so. A woman needing to hear the word of the Lord? Certainly.

Jacob's well was on one side of the little town of Sychar, but the town had two wells. The other well, the Ain Askar, was on the other side of the town and was more commonly visited by the women and girls drawing water. Why did she come to Jacob's well? Perhaps she had been working in the fields close by, or her house was nearer Jacob's well than the well across town, or she chose this well because with her shadowed background she would rather avoid the other women and girls coming to draw water.

I find myself identifying with this woman's transaction with Jesus. I have been that way before. I acknowledge that my own heart is the ground where His words can take root and flourish into full growth, or where I can stifle their seeding and growth with monstrous weeds generated by my own sin. There is a lesson too for me in how the Lord brought this woman to faith. I find that my own trust in Him depends on my willingness to invite His intervention as the Word of God into the hidden away places I pride as my own.

The Beginning

We can be sure that Jesus will always take the initiative when He encounters a ready heart. The woman's heart was ready to receive His words, though He had to take her on a careful personal journey before faith appeared on the scene. "Jesus said to her, 'Will you give me a drink?'" (John 4:7). Open the door to dialogue. Step over her obstacle of racial discrimination. Find a way into the woman's heart. When He did she erected the first barrier. You are a Jewish man and I am a Samaritan woman; on these two counts this conversation should not be taking place. She was certainly listening, and that was the first requisite for trust to grow in her heart. However, His invitation for her to move towards trust in the Lord was not accepted. Stall in argument. Barren ground. Perhaps the adversary intercepted the Lord's words and let them die in mid-air.

The Appeal

He reached out to her a second time. His aim was faith, as it always is, and He is not put off by a stalled argument. "If you knew the gift of God and who it is that asks you for a drink, you would have asked him and he would have given you living waters" (John 4:10). Look beyond His well. There are greater truths than this stone parapet and the sweet water that lies below. There is a well that yields sweeter waters than these. If you seek it with all your heart it will become a living spring of eternal waters that will always leap up within you and joy will be there.

So take her one more step towards faith. Show her that there are differences between the values attached to the kingdoms of this earth, and the principles and values of the eternal kingdom. Go the way of human reason and you will be thirsty again. Follow the steps I am placing before your feet and you will find eternal life.

At last the seed is lodged. She has continued to listen even though her words and arguments suggested otherwise, and now the first glimmerings of a light begin to shine in the dark places of her heart in response to the words of the Lord. "Sir, give me this water so that I won't get thirsty and have to keep coming here to draw water" (John 4:15). With these first tentative steps towards faith, there is also ignorance—"and have to keep coming here to draw water."

We are such a mixture we human beings. We have our desire for the Lord locked away in the clutter of our own ignorance and need, as though we want to have the best of both worlds. Water that will always satisfy the deepest needs of our hearts, and the water that flows out of the broken and polluted wells of the world and seeks to find its way into our lives through cisterns that cannot hold any other kind of water.

The Confrontation

The Lord knew that the time had come for the woman to finally confront the issue that stood between her and the truth. "Go, call your husband and come back" (John 4:16). The Lord gave her the opportunity for honesty and she responded, "I have no husband," handing Him a statement that was both part of the truth but also obscured the truth. Jesus replied, "You are right when you say you have no husband. The fact is you have had five husbands and the man you now have is not your husband" (John 4:17, 18). What Jesus didn't say—for there was no need to say it—was that the Rabbis permitted only two or three divorces. Beyond that a relationship between a man and a woman bordered on adultery for which the punishment was stoning to death.

The woman then acknowledged a growing perception about the One leading her along the path to faith. "'Sir,' the woman said, 'I can see you are a prophet'" (John 4:19). Here she was using the word "prophet" in its Jewish sense; one who sees and hears what God is saying and then makes it known so that His people can believe. The woman knew that Jesus was listening to the Father.

How did the woman look at Jesus when He revealed how well He knew her? Did she look at Him with shame that her truth was known? Or did her face become hardened and her eyes opaque and suddenly distant? Had the Lord come too close and did she now have to divert His attention? Whatever her inner emotions and motives she abruptly changed the subject. Perhaps she directed the Lord's attention up the steep slope of Mount Gerizim when she said, "Our father worshiped on this mountain, but you Jews claim that the place where we must worship is in Jerusalem" (John 4:20).

I can understand all these ploys for they are as familiar to me as the woman's ploys would have been to the Lord. However, the Lord wasn't about to let her inner search for faith end in a futile argument about religion, which is where so many of us would have it end, and I, to my shame, with them. He who is Himself the Word of God would continue listening to the words that came from the Father and then speak into her mind and heart the words that were both spirit and life (see John 6:63). He knew there was good fertile ground within reach of His words.

The Challenge

He took up her challenge about the temple where Samaritans worshipped and brought before her His own challenge. He took what she believed and brought it together with what the Father required of His people, their worship. Such gentleness. No pressure. No compulsion for her to answer in a particular way or to espouse a doctrine that looked like the truth but that missed the mark entirely. Then He ended with the words that were His final challenge to her; "God is spirit, and his worshipers must worship in spirit and in truth" (John 4:24).

She had a last flutter with argument. "The woman said, 'I know that Messiah, (called Christ) is coming. When he comes he will explain everything to us'" (John 4:25). As if to say, "I can wait until then, before I have to listen to all the truth." She was putting off the moment of decision and commitment. Delaying the time when she would have to place her trust in the One who knew all things about her. Was the adversary attempting to steal away the words of the Lord before they could take root?

The Person

Then Jesus spoke His last words that leapt across argument and religion, and embedded themselves in the now fertile ground of her heart. All that had been said was leading the woman to this point when she confronted the person who invited her trust. Jesus said, "I who speak to you am he" (John 4:26). He had taken her past the shadows of her own background, avoided the labyrinthine alleys of religious argument, and faced her with the final Word of God; with Himself. There faith was born for she found she could indeed trust this strange Jew, as we can, for we know Him as Jesus of Nazareth, our Saviour and our Lord.

The Postscript

The women left her water jar and went back into the town where she told the people, "Come, see a man who told me everything I ever did. Could this be the Christ?" (John 4:29). They left the town with her and went to the well where Jesus was speaking with His disciples. John records that, "Out of that city many of the Samaritans [first] believed in Him because of the woman's testimony" (John 4:39, literal translation in Greek). Later when they themselves had spoken with the Lord they believed in Him because of the words He spoke into their own hearts. These Samaritans moved out of personal ignorance, past limited knowledge of their religion and beyond acceptance of what the woman had told them into their own relationship with Jesus.

The words "believe in" that John used to describe their faith are *pisteuo eis*. They are the same words we encountered in the previous chapter. There by Jacob's well, and later in the town, Jesus fulfilled who He is as the Word of God and brought to faith those men and women who heard His spoken words and allowed them to lodge in their hearts as seed in good ground. In them as in the woman, were fulfilled Paul's words, "Then the Faith [is] from hearing and the hearing through a word [*rhema*] of Christ" (Rom. 10:17, literal translation in Greek).

Conclusions

I know I am like the woman encountering the Lord by the well at Sychar. The pathways that He would have me tread that lead to the place where I can trust Him are long and often tortuous. I am often distracted by the different wells I have dug into this world's systems and have to skirt around the obstacles I unwittingly put in the way of self-surrendered trust. There are occasional clouds of doubt that obscure my way, and relationships that I try to believe promise so much but which inevitably fail to satisfy the daily hunger and thirst of my soul.

For me, as with the woman at the well, it is all about trust. When Jesus first spoke with her she had two choices. Walk away from this strange Jew, or stay at the well and listen to His compelling words. The first choice, had she made it, would have required nothing more from her than the strength to walk away with or without her water pot. The choice she did make had to involve trust in the One who asked her for water. She probably had no idea that her first tentative acceptance of the One who spoke with her would lead to that self-surrendered trust that was the objective of the words He spoke into her soul.

The Lord continued in conversation with the woman at the well. He would not be content until her faith reached the place where it could sustain her in her search. Every word He spoke was imbued with the gentle power of the Holy Spirit until His purposes, each relating to her own special needs, were achieved.

Like the woman I cannot escape the sounds of His voice. He confronts me at every turn in my search to discover what it means to believe. As I listen for the sounds of His words spoken by His Spirit into my spirit, I discover the same three purposes He had in mind when He spoke with the woman at Sychar so long ago. These purposes reach across the centuries and enfold me and all those who would believe in their gentle though deliberate grasp.

The first purpose of His words to me is to set me free from all the questions, arguments, and doctrines that focus my undivided attention on religion and distract me from the living Word of God. He brings me back again and again to Himself; for the Word of God is the only One able to fill the void within my soul.

The second purpose of His words to me is to direct my attention to the hidden things in my own life; to my misguided transgressions, my self will, the self-centeredness of my relationships, the selfish needs that pre-empt His will, and the motives that place my own interests above the wellbeing of those with whom I have to relate. I am comforted that He Himself also knows all the strange shadowed meanderings of my own soul and the inner obstacles I obstinately put in the way of self-surrendered trust in Him.

The third purpose of His words to me is to direct my attention to principles of faith that would serve me well in my own walk with my Lord. These are principles of trust, obedience, fellowship with the eternal Beings who inhabit eternity, prayer, joy, living waters, eternal life, worship, truth, and spirit. Each of the Lord's *rhema* is intended to take me beyond the stereotypes of church religion and the expectations of belonging in a church community. Instead He would have me give my undivided attention to the Lord who is the Word of God.

In speaking with the woman at the well Jesus fulfilled another of Paul's instructions, like an object lesson of a divine truth that holds to this day. "The servant of the Lord must not strive; but be gentle unto all men, apt to teach, patient, In meekness instructing those that oppose themselves; if God peradventure will give them repentance to the acknowledging of the truth" (2 Tim. 2:24, 25, KJV).

Jesus was leading the woman to faith but also to repentance. He wanted her to turn away from all that her old life offered and to turn towards the Word of God, the only One who would give her life and fill her days with meaning. This one eternal requisite of faith that comes by hearing His words ties the experiences of the woman by the well to myself and to all who would believe in Him in the twenty-first century. Repentance is the twin of faith. They give meaning to each other. As I complete the requirements of faith and repentance demonstrated by the Lord by the well in Sychar, my faith in the living Word of God will come to its daily consummation and beginning.

Chapter Five

Repent and Believe

The Beginning

I grew up with the words "repent" and "repentance." My first Bible teacher explained to me that these words refer to a change of direction; to a man or woman going down the road of life in one direction and then making an immediate about face and going in the opposite direction. Part of the doctrine of repentance I learned was that repentance marked the beginning of a person's walk into salvation. It is a kind of one off transaction essential for the forgiveness that washed away my sins and gave me entrance into His kingdom.

For a long time in my Christian life I had not ventured beyond these simple definitions and understandings. Not because I found the subject matter of repentance difficult, but rather because I had not taken the trouble to fully explore it with the Holy Spirit guiding me into this difficult of truths. Why difficult? Because as my search continued I found that repentance runs counter to all that I naturally expect of myself as a disciple of Jesus Christ.

Paul contrasted two kinds of sorrow in his second letter to the assembly at Corinth when discussing repentance: godly sorrow that works repentance, and sorrow of the world that brings death (2 Cor. 7:9, 10). I had not known there was a difference. Had I been guilty of the wrong kind of sorrow? Had I stepped away from the godly sorrow that brings repentance and indulged myself in the sorrow that brings death? Could I open my own heart to the sorrow that comes when sin is faced? I had to find out.

When I searched the Scriptures, I discovered that my study divided easily into two periods of history. The first period led the Jewish people to the coming of Jesus, the old covenant, and the second tracked Jesus through the three years of His life to His death, resurrection, and the coming of the Holy Spirit and beyond: the new covenant.

The Old Covenant: The King and the Housewife

The King went out onto the roof of his palace. He couldn't sleep; his mind was obviously full of the affairs of state. I can see him idly looking out over the house tops, perhaps wanting something to distract him from kingly matters, and of course he found it, or rather he found her. She stood on a nearby housetop, shed each of her garments, and began to bathe in full view of the king. Desire reached out its ungainly hand and lay hold of the body of the king. From that moment he was a lost man. The King was David. The housewife was Bathsheba.

From the moment when sin was born, repentance became a necessity. We all know the story that involved adultery and then murder. The record simply states, "But the thing David had done displeased the Lord" (2 Sam. 11:27). Therein laid the foundation of his repentance. There were four people involved, not three. It was not simply David, Bathsheba, and Uriah. The Lord of glory was there that evening.

The Lord sent Nathan the prophet to David with a parable about the man who owned only one ewe lamb. He had raised the lamb himself and it was like a daughter to him. Along came a rich man who took the poor man's ewe lamb, killed it, and prepared a meal for a visitor. When David heard the parable he was angry and told Nathan that the man who had done this deserved to die and must pay for the ewe lamb four times over. The prophet looked at David and said, "You are the man!" (2 Sam. 12:7). So the Lord confronted David with his transgression.

I know that inner voice well and the shame that follows after a sin against the Lord or against another person. Shame is different from condemnation, though I know how to damn myself without walking in sorrow to the cross. His voice is like the still small voice the Lord used to speak with Elijah at the entrance to the cave (1 Kings 19:12). It is clear, precise, and does not need long explanation. His words leading me to repentance are as terse as Nathan's words to David. "You are the man!"

Nothing is said about what went through David's mind when he heard those words and the Lord's detailed denunciation that followed. However, when Nathan had finished speaking David confessed, "I have sinned against the Lord" (2 Sam. 12:13). We note that David didn't say that he had sinned against Bathsheba or her dead husband Uriah. It was the Lord he had sinned against.

The Lord's response to David's remorse was swift and precise. He gave Nathan the words that were like a *rhema* we explored in the previous chapter. "The Lord has taken away your sin. You are not going to die" (2 Sam. 12:13).

There is no reference to David's gratitude for the peace that the Lord's forgiveness would have produced. It is only hinted at in the psalm that commemorates this event. He wrote, "O Lord, open my lips, and my mouth will declare your praise" (Ps. 51:15). Was David praising the Lord for His forgiveness and for the peace that forgiveness brings? I believe so. However, there is a postscript written in tears.

I imagine David faced a personal inner conflict that involved his remorse at having sinned against the Lord and having brought about the death of Uriah. Thankfulness and sorrow. Sunshine and shadow. David's continued remorse is the companion of repentance. It is the shadowed counterpart of the peace that the Lord's forgiveness brings.

David's sin has been taken away, but in spite of the wonder of the Lord's mercy the memory of that sin could never be removed from the intricate networks of David's brain. Sorrow remained. He wrote, "For I know my transgressions, and my sin is always before me" (Ps. 51:3), and, "Restore to me the joy of your salvation" (Ps. 51:12).

I am on such familiar ground. As I look back through countless experiences lived over many years I encounter the catalogue of sins I have committed against the Lord and against His people. Like David I know them all, even though they are all forgiven (see Ps. 103:2). Yet I take refuge in the words David spoke before the Lord, "As far as the east is from the west, so far has he removed our transgressions from us" (Ps. 103:12), and then to Jeremiah, "For I will forgive their wickedness and will remember their sins no more" (Jer. 31:34).

One of my responses to these memories of sin is, "How could I have been so blind and so stupid and so ignorant?" When I ask those unnecessary questions I find myself facing two doors: one marked "guilt," and the other marked "self-condemnation." Even more, beyond those deceptively inviting doors there is a self-imposed darkness that delights in keeping alive the terrible pain of sin. Grief over forgiven sins is not darkness. It is a wonderful counterpart of the light that shines from the Lord's heart into my own. Perhaps it is part of the godly sorrow that Paul wrote about.

What began in shame on the rooftop when David let desire work its evil, flowed through all the stages of repentance, forgiveness, and gratitude when the relationship with the Lord was restored. His sin was taken away. His grief remained.

The Old Covenant: Law and Faith

As I reflect on this event in David's life I am confronted by two principles that form the background to his repentance. The first is obedience to the law. The second is trust in the Lord.

David would have known each of the Ten Commandments that God revealed to Moses on Mount Sinai. He had broken three of them; "You shall not murder" (Ex. 20:13). "You shall not commit adultery" (Ex. 20:14). "You shall not covet your neighbor's wife, or his manservant or maidservant, his ox or donkey, or anything that belongs to your neighbor" (Ex. 20:17).

One of my definitions of sin relates this wayward and self-fulfilling activity to the laws we sin against. Sin is, "behaviour that runs contrary to God's laws." Paul when writing to the assembly at Rome, declared, "I would not have known what sin was except through the law. For I would not have known what coveting really was if the law had not said, 'Do not covet'" (Rom. 7:7).

David's three sins were defined by the law, which also formed the basis for his repentance. Turn away from coveting his neighbour's wife. Turn away from adultery. Turn away from murder. These laws were like the starting blocks out of which sin had burst into life. Now they had to become the finishing line at the end of David's path to repentance. Obedience to the laws had to be restored. Of course it was too late to undo the outcomes of sin. Uriah was dead, the woman with whom he had committed adultery would continue to sleep in his bed, the child of Bathsheba would die, and there were human and divine consequences of his acts as Nathan had reminded him. The blood he had shed would continue to haunt his house and family (see 2 Sam. 12:10–14).

There was another transgression that David was guilty of. It is not defined by the Law of Moses. Instead it is an integral part of David's relationship with his Lord. Nathan reported the Lord's words to David. "I gave your master's house to you, and your master's [Saul's] wives into your arms. I gave you the house of Israel and Judah. And if all this had been too little, I would have given you even more" (2 Sam. 12:8). What Nathan did not say was something like this, "Why didn't you trust me to provide for all your needs? Why did you need to resort to the ways of the sinful flesh when all the resources of heaven were at your disposal? Why did you let the ways of the world infiltrate your thinking when you are a citizen of another kingdom?" Why indeed!

David had substituted reliance on his own wilful desires for trust in the God who had anointed him with oil as the future king of Israel and who had delivered Goliath into his hands. With Bathsheba, David's self-gratification replaced his trust in the Lord who had given him so much. The failure to trust his God was David's sin. The return to trust had to be one of the outcomes of David's repentance, though trust, curiously enough, is not defined by the law of Moses.

In the Scriptures we find echoes of David's understanding that trust and repentance were two parts of the same spiritual package. In Psalm 32 he wrote of sin, repentance, and forgiveness. "Then I acknowledged my sin to you and did not cover up my iniquity I said, 'I will confess my transgressions to the Lord'—and you forgave the guilt of my sin" (Ps. 32:5). In the same psalm he also declared that, "the Lord's unfailing love surrounds the man who trusts in him" (Ps. 32:10). Trust that the Lord would hear his cry of repentance. Trust that the Lord would forgive him. Trust that the Lord's love would not be taken from him.

In the events that followed that unexpected sight on the rooftops, the Lord's compassion and love joined together with David's repentance and trust, and forgiveness was born. I know these principles of repentance for they reach across the centuries and find their lodging place in my own heart.

The principles of repentance that applied to David under the old covenant are disturbingly clear. But do they carry over into the new covenant?

Transition: Repentance with John and Jesus

Records of this first period of our study are sparse, but there is a remarkable similarity between what John the Baptist taught and what the Lord and His disciples taught. Both were calls to repentance by those seeking forgiveness (see Mark 1:4; Mark 6:12, although there is no record in the Lord's teaching that forgiveness followed repentance). The call to repentance was accompanied in both cases by baptism (see Luke 3:3; John 4:1). Also, in both cases repentance was connected to the kingdom of God (see Matt. 3:2; Matt. 4:17).

Repentance in the life of David had its origins in transgressions defined by the law. However, with John the Baptist there seems to be a shift away from this principle. The law is not mentioned in John's teaching. Instead he gave four examples of repentance in action. "The man with two tunics should share with him who has none, and the one who has food should do the same." To the tax collectors he said, "Don't collect any more than you are required to." Also to the soldiers he gave three instructions. "Don't extort money and don't accuse people falsely—be content with your pay" (see Luke 3:11–14). How was sin defined in these instructions? What was there to be forgiven? Where was repentance?

When I examined each of John's teachings I found myself looking at quite a different kind of sin. Not the sins David committed, but something much more intangible, more personal, more difficult to define. I find three categories of sin embedded in John's teaching, and each of them applies to me.

The first involved repentance of a lifestyle focused on self and self-gratification. Share what you've got with others. Don't let them be unprotected from the cold. Don't let them go hungry. Repent of living only for yourself and being satisfied when your own needs are met. Be aware of others who also have needs.

When John directed his attention to the tax collectors the same principles emerged, but in this case it was selfishness run rampant. Many tax collectors used their legal contracts with the Roman authorities to extort and bribe the populace while becoming rich in the process. As with Matthew the tax collector, the message would have been "repent of your criminal lifestyle where desire drives the accumulation of money by any means."

Repentance of injustice also emerged in John's teaching. Don't use your power to generate fear in others and thereby extort money. As well as, don't use the same power over others because you are a tax collector or because you are a soldier with a sword and can accuse people falsely without any fear of being held accountable. It is likely that such unjust acts—though this is not stated—arose out of discontent driven by the self-centred drive to acquire what the world calls "the good things of life," always at the expense of others.

Repentance for John did not begin with transgressions against the law but with the lifestyle that does not reach beyond the gratification of one's own selfish desires. Repentance I began to see begins with what is buried within one's heart and soul. Ouch!

Jesus didn't explicitly explain the nature of repentance but these same principles apply in much of what He taught. The Lord certainly addressed the lifestyle that majored on selfishness and injustice. On relationships, Jesus taught that if a man's brother has something against him he should go to that brother and be reconciled before attending to his religious duties (see Matt. 5:23, 24). On the needs of others He said, "when you give to the needy do not announce it with trumpets" (Matt. 6:2). On the selfish accumulation of wealth, Jesus instructed the rich young man who came to him inquiring about the kingdom of heaven, "Go, sell your possessions and give to the poor" (Matt. 19:21). Also, in a telling application of these principles, "Do not judge, and you will not be judged. Do not condemn, and you will not be condemned. Forgive, and you will be forgiven. Give, and it will be given to you" (Luke 6:37, 38).

Had something changed in God's administration of sin and repentance between the times of David and John the Baptist? Neither John nor the Lord refers to the law as the basis for sin and repentance. Was I missing something? Then it dawned on me. Sin as an offence against our God had not changed. Repentance as a turning away from something and a moving towards something else had not changed. It was the kingdom and the laws of the kingdom that had changed.

The New Covenant: The Kingdom of God

David understood "kingdom" to mean the land and people over whom he ruled. For both John and Jesus the concept changed. "Kingdom" now referred to the kingdom of God. David's repentance functioned in the earthly kingdom of Israel and was determined against the laws of that kingdom. Could it be that if I wanted to understand my own sin and repentance I had to look into the laws of this other kingdom? Also could it be that these laws would define both my sin and give direction to my repentance?

The kingdom of God—*basileia tou theou*—is the royal dominion where the eternal laws of God are known and obeyed, the rule of the King, the administration of the affairs of His kingdom, the rule of divine law and the administration of divine justice.

Now my world turned upside down. What I had so innocently taken for granted about sin and repentance—obedience to law—had been challenged. I had to take this new part of my search as far as it would let me go. I had three basic questions that if I could find the answers to could tell me how I had to live as His disciple and as a subject of this new kind of kingdom. Where was the kingdom of God? What were its laws? What place had my repentance in His kingdom?

A group of Pharisees came to Jesus with the question, "When would the kingdom of God come?" They looked for the day when Roman administration would be replaced by the rule of Israel by a Jewish king. It is against this understanding that we read Jesus' reply. "The kingdom of God does not come with your careful observation, nor will people say, 'Here it is,' or 'There it is,' because the kingdom of God is within you" (Luke 17:20, 21). The better translation is, "The kingdom of God is among you; in your midst."

His kingdom has no boundaries. There is no capital city. It has no relations with the kingdoms of the world and does not receive ambassadors or make treaties with other kings. When faced with a similar question by Pilate, Jesus replied, "My kingdom is not of this world" (John 18:36).

The kingdom of God is populated by men and women whose membership in the kingdom is also unseen. Its citizens are those who have been born into the kingdom by the Father conferring His own spiritual genetic code on those who become His sons and daughters. Without that inner birth there would be no subjects and no kingdom. It begins within the one who believes and whose heart is changed forever. Its boundaries expand as more and more people travel the same narrow path to forgiveness and discipleship.

If we look at Christians as Samuel did when he went to Jesse's family to anoint one of his sons as a king, we will fall into error. The shape of man, his bodily features, his youth or age, his human attributes and qualifications cannot tell you whether this one or that one is a subject of God's kingdom. Position, status, and human authority have nothing to do with it. Nor do the things we are assigned to do in church, the vestments we wear or do not wear, or the contributions we make to the church's programmes. Nor does wealth, the prestige that wealth buys, success in education or business, or the control of super large churches relate to position in the kingdom of God. The subjects of this kingdom are men and women who have born again hearts that belong to the Lord who purchased them, and whom are subject to the immediate rule of the King.

The New Covenant: The Laws of the Kingdom

Like the kingdom of Israel, I was sure that the kingdom of God would have its own laws. Looking into the future of the earthly kingdom of Israel, Jeremiah prophesied that He would make a new covenant with them and promised, "I will put my law in their minds and write it on their hearts" (Jer. 31:33; see also Heb. 10:16). Jeremiah was looking far down the parade of years to the end when Israel would be re-gathered to her own land and the King Himself would in person rule over them. However, the prophecy also has a more immediate fulfilment.

God's laws in this age of grace have taken on a different form and style. It is against these laws of the kingdom that my sins must be known and my repentance defined. The first law defines all the rest. Paul wrote that bearing one another's burdens fulfils "the law of Christ" (Gal. 6:2). Now I'm in unidentified territory. Part of me wants to compare this law to all the other laws that kept the children of Israel in line. Written in stone and kept in the holy silence of the tabernacle. But I can't. They were written down. This is not.

The nearest I can come to the law of Christ is to say that it represents all that Jesus taught such as in the Sermon on the Mount. However, that is not entirely satisfactory. For just as the law of gravity is expressed in actual falling objects, the movement of the earth around the sun, and the steps I take along the pavement, so the law of Christ was expressed in the life Jesus lived both here on this circumscribed earth and there in that limitless heaven.

This law of Christ has another dimension that I cannot take lightly or dismiss as convenient doctrine. The One who is an expression of this law, Jesus the Christ Himself, and who is seated at the right hand of the Father, has also taken up His residence within my spirit where He expresses His laws, the laws of His kingdom—"which is Christ in you the hope of glory" (Col. 1:27). The law of Christ is within me. How extraordinary that the God of glory should come to this most fallible human and imperfect mortal, and there write His law within my own heart.

When I stand in the shadow of His eternal truth I am able to define my sin in two ways. Firstly, sin is my failure to recognise and acknowledge His presence in my heart. I can cope with the doctrine of His presence, for doctrine only touches my head and may not make any demands on my spirit unless I will it so. However, for the living, eternal, infinite Word of God who spoke and the heavens were spread out in space, for this One to dwell and to be at rest within me is almost impossible for me to deal with.

I find myself struggling with the living truth of Paul's words to the assembly at Colosse. He wrote, "My purpose is that they may be encouraged in heart and united in love, so that they may have the full riches of complete understanding, in order that they may know the mystery of God, namely Christ, in whom are hidden all the treasures of wisdom and knowledge" (Col. 2:2, 3). All those infinite and eternal treasures are hidden in Him and He is hidden in my heart.

Secondly I can define my sin against the law of Christ as my failure to open the ears of my spirit to hear and to heed what He is telling me from within. It is sin if I don't, can't, or won't listen. It is sin if I fail to receive those hidden treasures of wisdom and knowledge that He has promised. Also, it is sin when I do receive them and they remain like kernels of grain on the surface of a stony heart that does not give them entrance.

Maria was a woman we had befriended. She was divorced and had a son who was as use to following his own way as he was to breakfast. It was not unusual for Maria to report that Joseph had punched a hole in the bedroom wall or that he sat for hours transfixed by a seemingly endless series of computer games. Maria wasn't exempt from the same self-willed and destructive way of life. She would confess to having little money or having spent it on her own desires, which were many. However, when it was pointed out that she could trust the Lord for all her needs and turn her back on a life filled with her own gratification, she seemed not to hear. All that we said seemed only to reinforce her distance from the Lord. Her heart was shut. Her inner ears could not hear. For Maria, repentance was impossible.

Within this law of Christ are all the other laws of the kingdom that define my sin and repentance. These include the law of faith (Rom. 3:27), the law of liberty (James 1:25), the royal law, the law of love (James 2:8), the law of the Spirit of life (Rom. 8:2), and the law of righteousness (Rom. 9:31). All are carried under that one heading, the law of Christ. For He, in His person, lived out each one and will now enable me as His disciple to obey these same laws of His kingdom in the world.

The New Covenant: The Shape of My Repentance

Now I can begin to feel the shape of my daily repentance. It is not defined by the external laws as was David's repentance: murder, adultery, covetousness, and then his failure to trust his Lord. It is defined by the heritage I have as a child of the living God. It is defined by the law of Christ I am called to obey. It is defined by the presence of the Holy One of God within my reborn spirit.

My daily repentance requires that I turn away from all that would distract me from this most demanding and precious way of faith. It requires that I turn back to the One who lives within me. Turn back to what He will disclose of Himself and His ways upon the earth. Turn back to obedience, service, trust, love, and the bondage of freedom I owe the One who died for me.

There is one more amazing dimension of the Father's life within me. Paul expressed it in a question to the assembly at Rome. "Do you show contempt for the riches of his kindness, tolerance and patience, not realizing that God's kindness leads you toward repentance?" (Rom. 2:4). How dare I insult His kindness? How can I ignore His patient call to repent?

This part of my search is nearly over and I can begin to identify what repentance means. Repentance from my failure to trust. Repentance from the bondages I so easily wrap around myself like the gluey strands of s spider's web. Repentance from my failure to love another, when I replace love with all the insulting demands of my old nature: condemnation, failure to listen, refusal to bear another's burdens, and refusal to declare the word of the Lord to them. Repentance from my refusal to engage the spirit of Life within me, relying instead on the demands of my old sinful nature. Finally, repentance for the unrighteous words, deeds, and attitudes that have their roots well hidden in that same old nature.

Perhaps the most daunting task I find as I seek to know and apply daily repentance as part of my life of faith is what Paul referred to in his letter to the Ephesians. As though he had me in mind, Paul summed up the essence of repentance. He wrote, "You were taught, with regard to your former way of life, to put off your old self, which is being corrupted by its deceitful desires; to be made new in the attitude of your minds; and to put on the new self, created to be like God in true righteousness and holiness" (Eph. 4:22–24).

Not only does Paul provide the essence of my repentance, but he also states its goal, "to be like God." Can I cope with that challenge? Do I have the resources in myself so that my new man can be progressively changed into the image of the Creator? In myself? No! Never! Not in a million years! The truth was expressed in Paul's words, "But we have this treasure in jars of clay to show that this all-surpassing power is from God and not from us" (2 Cor. 4:7). Therein is His grace expressed.

The repentance, to which He calls me, is as radical and comprehensive as that faced by Matthew sitting at his tax office when the Lord called him to follow. He stood up and in an instant of time walked away from all the old man held so dear. He left behind attachments to wealth, family, and the network of friends and colleagues who supported his corrupt lifestyle. Beneath all those external things Matthew must have repented of the deep seated attitudes and values on which his lifestyle had been so painstakingly constructed.

Daily the Lord calls you and me to make repentance an inner attitude of mind, heart, and will. In so doing we will fulfil all that our Lord requires of us as His disciples as we face the twenty first century. Soon He will return to rule this earth and its people, and in person administer the laws of His kingdom on earth. Now He rules in the invisible kingdom of God that lives in those who repent and believe.

Chapter Six

God of the Impossible

My Own Journey

My own life has been a journey as a pilgrim across a land I thought I knew well. Touching foot in four continents, I have considered other religious philosophies, watched men and women worship in different religions, offer incense, kneel adoringly before family altars, pray to beings they could neither see nor hear, place flowers, flavoured rice, and coins on altars bedecked in garish colours hoping that the gods they worshipped would favour them. However, those systems of belief and legend reaching back into the mists of history promised no reality. They could teach me nothing about truth, wisdom, or redemption.

Also out of the mists of time one remarkable and extraordinarily human person emerged whose journey was so like the journey of all of us who would be His disciples. I have followed Abraham, the father of faith, through the trauma of uncertainty and opposition as he faced the challenges of faith and walked and spoke face to face with the One who makes all things possible. The principles of that ordinary yet extraordinary life are the same for disciples of all ages. Certainly for those of us who long to see the signs and wonders that displayed the power and authority of the Lord in the first century. We begin in the land of the Sumerians on the Euphrates River.

Abraham's Background

Terah named his son Abram. The Lord later renamed him Abraham. The record tells us that he began his journey in the city of Ur in the land of the Chaldeans where the Euphrates and Tigris Rivers flowed south into the Arabian Gulf. In that city he grew up with the smell of incense, the sights of robed priests, and the sound of temple music from the shrine to the moon god on top of the ziggurat.

The Scriptures tell us that the Lord called Abraham out of Ur of the Chaldeans to begin the long journey to Canaan. But where was Ur of the Chaldeans? The Hebrew word Ur can be translated either as city or region. Ur, city of the Chaldeans, or Ur, region of the Chaldeans. To make my search more difficult I find that Abraham's father Terah lived "on the other side of the flood in old time" (Joshua 24:2, KJV). "The flood" is the Euphrates River. The "other side of the flood" refers to the lands on its eastern banks. The city of Ur however is on its western bank. Did Abraham grow up in the city of Ur of the Chaldeans or in the land of the Chaldeans? Opinions are divided. In this study for simplicity's sake I have referred to Abraham's birthplace and the place where he grew up as the "city of Ur of the Chaldeans." The reader is encouraged to develop his own opinion.

Ur was an opulent city. Its harbour was open to vessels from the upper Euphrates and from towns and cities on what is now the Persian Gulf. Excavations have revealed palatial two storey houses lining well paved streets all within view of the Ziggurat and its silver shrine where the Sumerians worshipped Nannar the moon god. All around the city the fields of barley, wheat, and millet stretched beside their irrigation canals to the river as far as the eye could see. Alternating with the crops of grain were fields of vegetables that included peas, lentils, onions, garlic, and even cucumber. It was a rich land where Abram lived with his wife Sarai—she was also his half-sister—and he enjoyed a most comfortable lifestyle.

Abram's ancestors came originally we believe from the north, from what is now Armenia where his ancestor Shem, son of Noah, settled after the flood. From there some of Shem's descendants—Abraham's ancestors—moved south and settled on the Plain of Shinar in what was once the kingdom of Nimrod where Babylon was erected to prove that man was equal or superior to God.

At some point in the history of Abram's people their religious faith became separated into two streams. One stream acknowledged the God who accompanied Adam and Eve out of the Garden of Eden. The other, the corrupted stream, became founders and adherents of the religion of nations such as the Sumerians among whom Abraham lived.

I had long believed that Abram knew the one true God and trusted and worshipped Him, but Joshua tells me otherwise. Speaking to the assembled people at Shechem he said, "Long ago your forefathers, including Terah the father of Abraham and Nahor lived beyond the River and worshipped other gods" (Joshua 24:2).

Reluctantly I had to acknowledge that Abraham was probably very familiar with the idolatrous rites that attended worship of the gods and goddesses of the Chaldeans, known to historians as the Sumerians. Did Abram begin his journey of faith while worshipping in this corrupt religion? Did he have to come out of idolatry when God called him? The record seems to confirm these assumptions.

If this is true then the call of Abram is so like my own call. While I was deeply involved in the ways of the world He gave me the choice; obey the Lord's call; come out of darkness into light. There were no gods and goddesses in my world, but there was certainly plenty of idolatry (see Col. 3:5).

In the land of the Chaldeans Abram would have owed his allegiance to a multitude of gods and goddesses. At the head of their pantheon there were four great deities—three gods, one goddess—as well as a multitude of lesser gods such as the god of the pickaxe, the god of the brick mould, a god of beer, a god of dykes and ditches, the god of the sun, and the goddess of the moon.

The supreme being Abraham would have likely worshipped was An, the heaven god who ruled over all things. He was a shadowy being without any real identity in the pantheon. Under him was Enlil, the god of the air, "king of heaven and earth" and "king of all the lands." He was responsible for the creation, through his spoken word, of the productive features of the earth. In the supreme deity of An, and in Enlil, we see mockeries of the Father of all things and of the Lord Himself. The parallels are too obvious to be ignored. However, there is more.

Enlil was attended by Enki who was the god of wisdom and was responsible for organising the earth. Enlil made the general plans. Enki carried them out. In this Sumerian god I find a corruption of Adam who had been created to till the earth and rule over it. I believe that the first man—our own ancestor—would have been elevated to the status of godship by the later generations who revered his memory as the man God had created. After Babylon Adam became known as Enki. This process of deification still operates today. I once stood before the shrine of a Japanese emperor to whom people bring offerings and before whom they pray for divine blessings.

The fourth deity was the mother goddess, Ninhursag who was also known as Ninti, the lady who gave birth. When I read the Scriptures I find that "Adam named his wife Eve, because she would become the mother of all the living" (Gen. 3:20). It is not hard to imagine that the descendants of Eve, under the adversary's prompting, corrupted the nature of Eve and elevated her to be the mother goddess. The Sumerians worshipped her as Ninhursag, whom they regarded as the mother of all mankind and the one who began the chain of births that established humankind. Archaeologists at a large number of sites throughout the Middle East have unearthed many thousands of figurines, many with gross features suggesting fertility and motherhood. It could be that the figurines point back to the same human origin, the deification and worship of Eve.

These four gods were often listed together and were given places of honour at religious banquets and festivals that Abram could have attended. In these practices we find the corruption after Babylon of the pure religion given to Adam and Eve in the garden. The belief in one true God was distorted through the lies of the adversary so that faith became religion. The adversary doesn't fear religion. It is one of his tools in controlling mankind.

The First Challenge to Faith: Other Gods

Why did the Lord choose Abram when he worshipped other gods? Why does the Lord choose any of His disciples and call us out of the world? Nehemiah gives us one answer. He wrote. "You found his [Abram's] heart faithful to you" (Neh. 9:8). Even in that idolatrous place with the chants of prayers and the smell of incense from the painted temple on the top of the ziggurat, Abraham made the choice that all his future choices depended on. He opened his heart to the Lord his God who makes all things possible.

Recently a disciple I know well confided in me that the Lord had told him, "Your heart is mine." I note that the Lord didn't say, "Your life is mine," or "Your business is mine." The words were, "Your heart is mine." I can imagine the Lord using those words to Abram in the midst of his false religion. "Don't give your heart to these false gods. Your heart is mine." Abram's first choice was to surrender his heart to the God who had made him. For I believe it was on the basis of that surrender that Abram and his family walked out of the city gates where he had spent so much of his life, and began the long journey towards the land that God would show him.

There are so many attractive things in my world, attractive from a purely human point of view, and all of them make insidious demands on my heart's allegiance. So many world noises! So many voices that call me to serve them! Yet I hear the Lord's words in His prayer to the Father, "They [His disciples. You and I] are not of the world, even as I am not of it" (John 17:16).

Jesus has also made it clear that the primary reality is within the heart. I know that my own heart can so easily be blinded and hardened so that even though I can hear His words I cannot understand them and find trust. Without trust from the heart, not simply from the mind, I cannot be changed into the man where faith is singularly at home (see John 12:40, KJV, where the word "converted" means "to change and become as it were, another person").

Abram could not leave Ur until he had broken the tedious connections between his heart and the religious world that wanted him to yield his heart's obedience (see Rom. 6:16). With his repentance from the worship of those other gods and his heart's surrender, Abram responded to the first challenge to his faith. When he left Ur his heart truly belonged to the Lord.

The Second Challenge to Faith: The Settled Lifestyle

It would have taken him many days to cover the thousand kilometres from Ur North West before they saw the walls of Haran. This city, although devoted to the worship of Sin, the moon god, would also have been a family centre for Abram.

At Haran Abram interrupted his journey to the land God had promised him.

There he, Sarai, and Lot stayed for a considerable time (see Gen. 11:31, 32). Time enough for him to acquire men and women servants, flocks of sheep and goats, and shepherds to look after his flocks. Abram settled in Haran, put down roots, established his lifestyle as a herder of sheep and goats, and above all, made money.

Why did Abram interrupt his journey to Canaan and settle in Haran? All we have are the very emphatic words of scripture that perhaps hide a multitude of reasons. "But when they came to Haran, they settled there" (Gen. 11:31). The telling word, for me, is "but." It highlights an emphatic interruption in Abram's journey of faith to the land of Canaan. In Haran he broke the sequence of the journey God had instructed him to take. Was this interruption because of something personal? Did he question his first call to leave Ur of the Chaldeans to go to Canaan? (Gen. 11:31). Had his trust in the Lord God failed him? Did the attractions of life in the city of his fathers prove too much for Abram who was then in his seventies? Also, had his wife pressured him to choose the settled lifestyle in Haran rather than the traumas of a long arduous journey into a land she had never seen? There are no answers, only speculations.

It was in this settled lifestyle that we encounter God's second instruction, "Leave your country, your people and your father's household.... So Abram left as the Lord had told him" (Gen. 12:1, 4). Nothing could be more explicit. Abram had to say good-bye to his settled lifestyle and take on the way of life of a pilgrim. In his responses to the Lord we encounter the first indication of Abram's unquestioning and unconditional trust and surrender to the word and will of his Lord.

What is unwritten in the sacred record, but which challenges my own heart, are the words I imagine the Lord could have said to Abram, "Trust me enough to interrupt your settled lifestyle. Put trust and obedience to my command before any pleasant satisfaction that goes with living among family and friends. I am first. You gave me your heart in Ur. Your heart is mine. Now I am calling for your obedience to accompany that gift."

Abram obeyed the Lord, and his journey of faith, which the attractions of a settled lifestyle in Haran had interrupted, resumed.

I am challenged by the words of my Lord to His Father in that upper room. "For they are not of the world any more than I am of the world" (John 17:14). Like Abram I had once put down roots in this world, established my reputation in education, built a travel business, became accepted in certain international circles, served the world's institutions, and grew comfortable with a settled lifestyle. I knew all about the attractions of a settled lifestyle. For me leaving that way of life would have once seemed impossible.

The writer to the Hebrews acknowledged that Abraham, like so many others, admitted that they were strangers and pilgrims on the earth" (see Heb. 11:13, KJV).

Also, Peter who knew what he was talking about took up the same theme when he referred to his readers in the first century as, "strangers and pilgrims" (see 1 Peter 1:11, KJV). For so many years of my life I didn't know the real meaning of those disturbing words, "strangers and pilgrims."

If I am to take anything from this study of Abraham it will be this disturbing challenge of faith. Abraham did not belong in this world. Neither do I. None of us do unless we make that choice as Abram did when he arrived and settled in Haran. If we choose dependence on a settled lifestyle in the world rather than dependence on the One who calls me to pilgrimage, we fail in our faith.

The Third Challenge to Faith: Do It Yourself Religion

The Lord had promised Abram, "I will make you into a great nation" (Gen. 12:2), and a nation is identified both by its citizens and by the land the citizens occupy. After Abraham arrived in Canaan the Lord affirmed this dual promise with the words, "To your offspring I will give this land" (Gen. 12:7).

The problem for Abram was twofold. He was a wandering shepherd owning no land and his wife was sterile. God's fulfilment of both promises—and the first depended on the second—was therefore impossible.

The other player in this unfolding drama was Sarai. Obviously she knew of the Lord's promise, "To your descendants I will give this land, from the river of Egypt to the great river, the Euphrates" (Gen. 15:18). Of course Sarai knew that the descendants the Lord spoke about depended on her and on her ability to conceive. In her womanly logic she thought of a way around the problem of her sterility so that at least one of God's promises could be fulfilled. "Go sleep with my maidservant; perhaps I can build a family through her" (Gen. 16:2).

This was not faith. This was determination to please her husband, and perhaps hidden in her words was Sarai's desperate wish to be the mother of nations and to see her husband fulfilled.

I wonder what they talked about in the privacy of their tent before sleep claimed them. Did they examine their situation over and over again, rolling it around in their minds like a pebble in a stream? Trying to justify Abram taking Hagar to bed and at the same time needing to acknowledge the Lord's promise?

Abram made the choice. He took Hagar to bed. A son was conceived and duly born. They named him Ishmael as God had instructed. This course of action was so logical, and I find the same logic prevailing in the church of the twenty-first century. We so often tell ourselves, God has given us the ability and the human resources to handle every situation. Even though we don't see the impossible happen we are so often content with small gains. Use what God had given us, even though we haven't heard from Him directly, and hopefully He will honour our efforts. Or will He?

The Fourth Challenge to Faith: Human Frailty

Thirteen years passed before God again spoke with Abram. If I had been in that situation I would have been greatly tempted to take refuge in the inner shadow I call unknowing, where faith doesn't function. I would be tempted to go about the demands of daily living and relegate God's promises to the too hard basket rather than face the sometimes human loneliness of trusting Him. It is possible that Abram, having once compromised his relationship with God and His promises by fathering a son through Hagar, became locked—as I would have been—in that failure to believe. There is no evidence that he attempted to undo the damage he had done to his own spirit and to Sarai's faith.

After thirteen years God again appeared to him and confirmed the promise and covenant. He then gave them new names. Abram he renamed Abraham "for I have made you a father of many nations," and Sarai He renamed Sarah, for she would be the mother of nations and kings of peoples would come from her (Gen. 17:5, 15, 16). The Lord then promised to Sarah that she would bear Abraham a son. At the time she was eighty nine years old. He was ninety nine. Abraham had two responses to the Lord and neither bears any resemblance to trust in the Lord Almighty.

On hearing the Lord's words, he fell face down and laughed. Clearly what God had said was impossible for it went against the natural processes that his and Sarah's bodies were capable of. His words express the difficulty as he saw it. "Will a son be born to a man a hundred years old? Will Sarah bear a child at the age of ninety?" The capacity for conceiving children disappears as the years accumulate. I would have found the Lord's words almost impossible to believe.

On that stumbling block of irrefutable logic my trust in the Lord, like Abraham's, would have faltered. Then, like Abraham, I would have fallen back on previous achievements, even though they had been in the flesh. So it was with Abraham; "If only Ishmael might live under your blessing" (Gen. 17:18). What you are saying Lord is obviously impossible. You must have a sense of humour after all, and you do have a backup option if your promises won't work.

How many times have I been in that position, if not consciously, at least by default, living as though the promises He has given me could not be achieved. I will never do greater things than He did. The lame won't be healed. The blind won't see. The paralysed and crippled can't possibly walk again. He won't reveal Himself by speaking into my benighted mind. My lack of faith leaves me with the other options, "If only Ishmael might live under your blessing." There are so many Ishmaels in my life (too many to count) as I am sure there are in yours. Just as Ishmael's conception and birth locked Abraham into that wilderness of unknowing for thirteen years, so my own Ishmaels turn me away from the Lord so that faith becomes as distant as yesterday's sunrise.

The Lord God did not rebuke Abraham for his unbelief nor did He chide Sarah when she laughed later at the entrance to her tent. He had announced that He would return after one year and that Sarah would have a son. Like Abraham, Sarah was probably taking refuge in the successful attempt they had already made to build a family by Hagar. As if to say, "We don't need you Lord." But of course they did, if His promises were to be fulfilled and He was to be faithful to what He had promised. In His grace He was not dissuaded by their unbelief. He never is. Nor does He chide me when I wander for days, months, and years in that wilderness of unknowing. He knows who I am and I will hear His call when my heart is open to receive Him.

Abraham defied the logic of aging bodies and took Sarah to bed. She conceived and one year later they both presented Isaac to the Lord of the impossible who had honoured His own word.

The Ultimate Challenge to Faith: Death

I have a catalogue of things I hold most dear. I won't bore you with details, but if you look carefully and honestly within yourself you will find a similar catalogue. People, places, objects, ideas, recreation, even occupations that we build our lives around and that we use as the basis for our contentment. Take something away and automatically, whether we like to admit it or not, we suffer the feeling of loss, grief, possibly resentment, and anger because something we cherished is no longer part of our established lifestyles. On a completely different scale God asked Abraham to give up his son who would have become a much cherished and inseparable part of their lives together. They would never have another son.

There are few records of Isaac's early years. At the age of eight he was circumcised and we know from the record that Sarah nursed him herself, impossible as that may seem. She confided to someone, "Who would have said to Abraham that Sarah would nurse children?" (Gen. 21:7).

When Isaac was weaned they held a great feast. There are no records of who was present, but at the feast or soon afterwards the first signs of antagonism between the brothers emerged. Ishmael mocked his brother. Sarah was distressed and told her husband to send the slave woman and her son away. He did, and Ishmael's separate line came into existence. He became an archer. His mother found a wife for him from her own Egyptian people and God promised that he would be the father of nations (see Gen. 21:9–20). Some suggest that the modern conflict between the Jews and the Palestinians can be traced to that ancient antagonism.

How old was Isaac when the Lord told Abraham to sacrifice his son, not any kind of death, but death at his father's own hand? We don't know. I have always had the idea that he was around twelve, but that cannot be confirmed from the Scriptures. We know that God required Abraham to sacrifice his son after he had made a treaty with Abimelech at Beersheba, and after he had been living in the land of the Philistines for a long time (see Gen. 21:22–34). What does "a long time" mean? Was Isaac twelve, fifteen, or about to leave the teenage years behind?

When they approached Mount Moriah Abraham referred to Isaac as "the boy." Not yet a young man, but old enough to know what sacrifice meant.

We know the story so well; the altar, the wood, Isaac bound for sacrifice, the knife to kill his son, the ram caught in the thicket, the voice of an angel. There in the loneliness of that place Abraham's faith came to full maturity. There he faced the ultimate challenge to trust in the God of the impossible—death itself—and walked away with his son alive and his faith recognised and honoured by the One he trusted.

There are so few records of Abraham's spiritual journey, but there on Mount Moriah we find two references that are like little portholes letting us look into the privacy of this man's faith. The first lets us look into his faith at that moment of greatest challenge. He told his servants, "Stay here with the donkey while I and the boy go over there. We will worship and then we will come back to you" (Gen. 22:5). This is trust in the God who delights in the impossible.

Here also we find a little bridge between the challenge Abraham faced and the victory his Father would unfold because of his faith. "We will worship." The sublime relationship between this man and his God, which had survived so much, was now reasserted in its full measure. We will worship. We will kneel before our Maker and acknowledge the supremacy of His ways, words, and promises. Our faith will come to its supreme expression. We will worship.

The second little window into Abraham's faith is found in what he said to Isaac when he asked his father, "Where is the lamb for the burnt offering?" (Gen. 22:7). Abraham's words leap across the centuries and enfold me in perhaps the deepest mystery of my own faith, "God himself will provide the lamb for the burnt offering" (Gen. 22:8). Death because of my sin is the ultimate challenge to my faith, but I exult in the God of my salvation who Himself is the Lamb of God who takes away my sin and clears my account with the Father. I will not die as sin promises. I will live in His company forever.

Renewing of Your Mind

Joshua recorded that "Long ago your forefathers, including Terah, the father of Abraham and Nahor, lived beyond the River and worshipped other gods"

(Joshua 24:2). We have named some of them in this chapter. When God brought Abraham out of Ur he had to leave behind the idols he had worshipped in Ur, but in one sense he brought them with him. All the evil practices that attended his worship of Nannar, Enki, and Ninhursag were securely locked away in Abraham's mind.

I cannot imagine what Abraham would have thought when he heard God's call to leave Ur and go to the land He would show him. Did he struggle with the challenge of this new knowledge of God placed on his old knowledge of other gods and goddesses? It may have been so, but over the years between his departure from Ur and his arrival at the great tree of Moreh at Shechem, Abraham would have securely lodged in his mind the knowledge that he served a different God. At Shechem he built his first altar to the Lord, and later a second one at Bethel (see Gen. 12:6–8). One God. One worship. One service.

Paul picked up this theme more than two thousand years later in words that seem to echo the experience of Abraham between Ur and Bethel. "Do not conform any longer to the pattern of this world [its gods and goddesses and the worship of the world's ways], but be transformed by the renewing of your mind. Then you will be able to test and approve what God's will is—his good, pleasing and perfect will" (Rom. 12:2).

Renewing: *anakainosis*, making different from what was previously there. Just as Abraham couldn't take his knowledge of the false gods with him so neither can I when I enter His kingdom. This is the greatest challenge I can face. Not simply to trust Him as a little child trusts, without questions and doubts and conditions, but with a trust built on the secure knowledge of who He is, and who I am, and the knowledge of the principles of faith and obedience He requires of me as His disciple.

I have to ask my very gentle yet stern Teacher to train my mind so that it can be renewed like the mind of a little child. A faith without questions. A faith untroubled by doubts. A trust I have not locked into prescriptions of religion, which are as implacable and unyielding as the rock of Gibraltar. A trust in the Lord like that only rises out of the heart and mind of a child.

Do I look back longingly and wish for signs, wonders, and miracles that will proclaim the Lord's sovereignty? If so I realise that I miss the point. I can't make signs and wonders happen. I can't somehow trigger the hand of the Lord to act with power and authority in the twenty-first century. I don't have the human authority to command the impossible. All I have is my own response to the Lord who asks that I submit to Him and to His careful training of mind and spirit as He would teach and train a little child.

The search is complete, but not the life that has to translate these principles of faith into daily living. I seek to trust Him as a little child trusts, without questions or doubts. I seek to understand Him as a little child understands Him, without doctrinal argument or rationalisation. I come daily and submit to His gentle renewing of my mind so that it can be made like His mind. like the mind of Christ (see 1 Cor. 2:16). I seek to relate to Him with the simplicity that accepts Him as He is and accepts myself as I am; warts and all. I believe that only that same self-surrendered trust and submission to Him, like that of a little child sitting at the Lord's feet, will bring my Lord to finally say, "Well done, good and faithful servant" (Matt. 25:23).

Chapter Seven

Obstacles

The Heart of the Matter

My trust in the Lord is one of the two essential elements in my life as Jesus' disciple (Rom. 1:17). The other essential is love. Without faith I cannot please the Father (Heb. 11:6). My trust in my Lord is fundamental to my salvation and entrance into the kingdom of the Father (John 3:15, 16). Also, it was my faith in the Son of God that enabled the Father to declare me righteous (Rom. 9:30).

I learned from the Apostle Paul that whatever I did, which did not have faith as its central ingredient, was sin. That's a fact; not an opinion (see Rom. 14:23). Even the sublime gift of eternal life of the eternal Son to express His own life in my own heart, is the Father's response to my unconditional trust in Him and my surrender to His Lordship (Eph. 3:17).

However, faith on its own is never enough. For faith and love belong together like twins from the same Father, as Paul reminded the disciples in the assemblies in Galatia, "For in Christ Jesus neither circumcision nor uncircumcision avails anything, but faith working through love" (Gal. 5:6, NKJV). Take away love, and faith becomes another sterile doctrine to be left on the shelf with all the other legal doctrines that cannot bring life. Take away faith, and love has no eternal amphitheatre to demonstrate the blessings of His grace. Try to live as Jesus' disciple without either faith or love, and discipleship degenerates into another faithless and loveless religion that the adversary welcomes, for in it we pose no threat to his evil ambitions.

With the great catalogue of faith the Scriptures present to us, we might think that the life of faith is a simple matter. However, if it were that simple, I ask myself, why haven't I been spared all the confusing and difficult experiences life puts in my path? Also, why do I find it so hard to walk a straight path of faith and obedience?

As every Christian knows, nothing about our life as disciples is straightforward, and so we come to the heart of the matter. There are very serious obstacles to my exercise of faith, and obstinate stumbling blocks to the act of trusting the Saviour. With that in mind I set out to learn what those obstacles to faith were and how I can experience the victory of faith over all that the adversary, the world, and the flesh would put in my way.

What are these obstacles to faith and where do they come from? Do they have their origin within the disciple? The unfortunate answer is, yes! Jude identified something within each of us he called "corrupted flesh" (Jude 23). Peter called the same inner presence "the sinful human nature" (2 Peter 2:18). John referred to it as "the cravings of sinful man" (1 John 2:16), and Paul gave it a number of names, "the flesh," (Rom. 8:4, KJV), "the body of sin" (Rom. 6:6), and "the old man" (Eph. 4:22).

The Scriptures also teach me that these inner realities are directly opposed to the Spirit that He gives us (see Rom, 8:6), and the Spirit is the source of our faith (Gal. 5:22). I come to two inescapable conclusions. The old man, my old unredeemed nature, by whatever name I know him, is the source of these obstacles to the exercise of my faith in the living Son of the Father. Also, faith is the resource the Father provides that enables me to overcome this most obstinate of adversaries which lies in wait to trip me up and keep me ineffective.

I wake up with my inner man every morning. It is almost as though the old man continues to brood when I am no longer conscious. I take the old man and the obstacles to faith he generates with me every time I make an excursion into the world. The world holds many attractions for the old man's unhealthy and depraved appetite and curiosity.

The old man came with Adam and Eve out of Eden. He troubled David who was a man after God's own heart. The old man in association with his great benefactor, the adversary, instilled hatred and confusion into the heart of Judas, and even the Lord's disciples weren't immune to his depredations. The voices and desires of the old man will continue to plague mankind until the Lord closes the age of grace with His coming again.

Jesus actually identified four of the inner obstacles to faith generated by the old man when He chided His disciples with the Greek word *oligopistos*, meaning, "of little faith." The Lord was the only one to use this unusual word and only in rebuke. The four situations His disciples faced, and which Jesus rebuked because they were contrary to faith, involved anxiety (Matt. 6:30), fear (Matt. 8:26), doubt (Matt. 14:31), and the failure to learn (Matt. 16:8). In this chapter I will examine two of these evil obstacles to faith—anxiety and fear—as they apply to my own life as Jesus' disciple.

Be Anxious for Nothing

Jesus had climbed a mountain in Galilee somewhere close to Capernaum and there He spent the night in fellowship with His Father. When morning came He called His disciples and chose twelve of them whom He named His apostles, envoys, and ambassadors. They were to be the representatives of His kingdom to carry His proclamations to the pagan kingdoms of the world.

In was probably early morning when He found a level place below the summit where His disciples gathered around Him. From that vantage point with the sun rising behind them they could see across the lower fields to the lake. On their left was the city of Capernaum where He spent so much time, and in the distance they could see the far shore of the lake His disciples knew so well. There the crowds inevitably found Him and probably sat in a great arc around the Lord and His disciples as He began to teach them some of the precepts of His own kingdom.

Today we call it the "Sermon on the Mount," but this term is not found in the original manuscripts. It was invented by Augustine around the year AD 400. Nor is it actually a sermon but rather a collection of the great teachings of our Lord. We conclude this because Luke has a parallel passage that does not include some of what Matthew records, and some of the things that Luke records are not found in Matthew. It is also interesting to note that Luke connects some of the passages in Matthew to times and places other than on the mountain. It is likely that both authors took a number of Jesus' teachings and arranged them in their own logical order to emphasize different facets of His kingdom.

It was in that unparalleled setting that Jesus explored one subject that goes to the heart of our faith and that earned the Lord's rebuke, "O you of little faith." The subject of His rebuke is anxiety (see Matt. 6:25–34).

I wonder who He was looking at when He began this teaching and what His disciples thought and felt when they heard the words, "Therefore I tell you, do not worry about your life, what you will eat or drink; or about your body, what you will wear" (Matt. 6:25). They could have felt that Jesus was speaking to each of them personally for they had all forsaken the ready income that provided the necessities of life. If anyone could have been open to anxiety about their daily needs, it was these twelve; though perhaps we can leave out Judas who had the money bag.

The Greek word Jesus used, and which is translated "worry," is *merimnao*, which means, "to be overwhelmed with the cares of life and of the world, to be filled with anxiety that divides the mind and distracts our attention from the higher priorities of the kingdom of God."

In this part of His teaching Jesus told His disciples that anxiety is futile. He pointedly asked them, "Who of you by worrying can add a single hour to his life?" (Matt. 6:27). I know what He was talking about. I can't count the number of times I have let a late arrival, a missing letter, a delayed phone call, a chance and unexplained remark, or even a sideways glance take me down the path into anxiety. I am very familiar with how the old man takes such unexpected events and blows them up into some kind of disaster. She's had an accident! He doesn't care! I've lost the job! The stock market will crash! I will be ruined! He doesn't trust me! So many of these imagined events fail to materialise when the time we were anxious about has come and long gone.

The Lord is clear about two alternatives to anxiety. The first is to trust the One who knows everything I need and who commands all the resources that give glory to the flowers and food to the birds. He told His disciples, "If that is how God clothes the grass of the field, which is here today and tomorrow is thrown into the fire, will he not much more clothe you, O you of little faith?" (Matt. 6:30). The unspoken principle is that we trust Him to do what is within His character to perform. His name after all is Jehovah Jireh; the Lord will provide. The Lord who provided a ram caught in a thicket on Mount Moriah where Abraham had gone to sacrifice his son, will clothe us and feed us if we trust Him with a whole heart.

The second principle embedded in this passage is that His disciples place the requirements of His kingdom above the compulsions of the old man and of the world. On that morning Jesus spelled out the stern and demanding priority for each of His disciples in every age; including me. "But seek first his kingdom and his righteousness, and all these things will be given to you as well" (Matt. 6:33). In the words of Jeremiah, the Lord requires that if I want to find Him I must seek Him with all my heart (see Jer. 29:13).

The Greek word translated "first" is *protos*, which means "the first in place, time, order and dignity." Jesus' statement turns me towards the place, which of all the places I attend to, comes first. It is the place where the life and laws of the kingdom are expressed. It is my own heart where the King would rule through His Spirit (see Luke 17:21). This is the place where He asks me to attend to all that is required of me as a citizen of His kingdom. It is in this holy inner place that His will can be known, where His love can be expressed (see Rom. 5:5), and where His joy will leap up like the fountain of life (John 4:13). Also, it is there in the innermost parts of my being that His inexpressible peace can stand guard over my heart and mind (John 14:27; Phil. 4:7).

The first thing I have to learn to seek is His kingdom and His righteousness before I focus on anything else in my day. Only in this way will I find the basis for any decision I need to make. I have learned, often to my cost, that my search must not be delayed by any activity or suggestion of the old man, certainly not by anxiety.

One day I had a visit from my boss late in the afternoon when everyone had gone home. He came into my office and sat in a spare chair obviously wanting to talk. We did; and the discussion came around to what I knew about the Lord, the cross, sin, forgiveness, and peace. I shared it all with him. Then, thinking that I could have said too much and intruded into his personal space I said, "Perhaps I've talked too much." His response, "No! I wanted to listen." As he left my office I heard him say again, "I wanted to listen."

My boss was a significant person in the world of education and would eventually become Director General of Education for the state we lived in. He was well thought of, enjoyed a rich—in worldly terms—lifestyle, and had an extensive network of friends. His response to my words that day would have evoked images of a change in his lifestyle and anxiety about what he would lose if he trusted the Lord and found his way to the door of the kingdom. Anxiety blocked his way to the door where the Lord was knocking. He could not seek first the kingdom of God no matter how clearly the Spirit had whispered into his heart that afternoon. He never did come to faith.

The word translated "first" also means the "first in order." On a scale of significance in my life as His disciple this stands at the very top of my list. There is nothing more significant than the inner movement of my will to seek His kingdom and righteousness. This search has priority above anything else in the sometimes confused and contrary agendas that seek to occupy my attention.

Finally the word "first" means "first in dignity." I challenge myself that if I want to hear the Lord honour me with His "well done good and faithful servant," then I will have to give myself, and all my energy and attention, into seeking and knowing the affairs of His kingdom and His righteousness (see Luke 19:17). He will only grace me with the dignity of an obedient servant when I fulfil these requirements.

Why righteousness? What is so important about the search for righteousness that the Lord gave it such a high priority?

As we know so well it is impossible for you and me to attain righteousness through our own actions, through obedience to any kind of legalism, through observance of religious ritual, through attendance at church as one of the favoured few, or through much prayer. All of these activities if done without love and the trust that accompanies love amount only to what the Scriptures call "works." However, righteousness is attributed to His saints by the Father. We can't work for it and it is never earned. As it was with Abraham, the Father attributes righteousness to those whose lives are on the line with unreserved trust in His Son (see Gen. 15:6; Gal. 3:5).

When I consider Jesus' teachings on that Galilee morning I am faced with a great contradiction. If I could stand anxiety and faith side by side I would find that both have their origin within my own heart. One comes naturally. The other has to be fought for. Anxiety, which introduces me to its ferocious twin fear, arises unbidden. It is the old man's prize—if I can use that word—for me when I attend to the voices I don't want to hear.

Faith on the other hand, has to be sought, earnestly, diligently, with all my heart, soul, mind, and strength. If I don't seek anxiety, I know it will relentlessly seek me out and find me. If I don't seek faith, it will always be a stranger to me and I will condemn myself to a lightless journey without hope.

I find that anxiety comes unbidden out of the old man who is hostile to God (see Rom. 8:7), and takes me down the familiar highway littered with all my failed attempts to live without trusting Him (Gal. 2:6). The old man can never please Him (Rom. 8:8). Faith on the other hand, which involves the sacrifice of my independence from the Lord, is a narrow path that takes me straight into His heart and favour (Heb. 11:6).

Why Are You so Afraid?

When Jesus came down from the mountain He was followed by large crowds without a shepherd and full of the most desperate needs. He soon encountered and healed a man disfigured by leprosy and then entered Capernaum where He healed the centurion's servant, cured Peter's mother-in-law, and cast out many demons. The Lord then climbed into a boat, probably belonging to one of His disciples, and asked that they cross over to the other side of the lake (Matt. 8:23–27).

At first the waters were calm and Jesus slept. Then a storm blew up across the lake and increasing in intensity, threatened to wash over them. The disciples were soon overwhelmed with fear and believed they were going to drown. I would of thought the same thing if I had been there. They woke Jesus, who needed only one look around to understand the two problems His disciples faced: the waves and their own faith. He replied with the gentle rebuke I have come to know so well. Matthew records; "He replied [to their cry], 'You of little faith, why are you so afraid?'" (Matt. 8:26).

There are two words in Greek for fear. The first is *phobos*, which is translated, "fear, terror, fright, dismay and which impels the frightened person to run away from that which causes fear." I have a mortal terror of spiders and will do anything to run away from them. This word *phobos* has entered our language in the shape of many phobias; agoraphobia, the morbid fear of open places; hydrophobia, the morbid fear of water; and monophobia, the morbid fear of being alone.

I had always thought that this was the kind of fear that earned Jesus' rebuke the phobia kind of fear. Jesus obviously knew His disciples were suffering from this very natural in-built capacity for self-preservation, but the word He used is much more damning and reveals an aspect of the old man that plagues all of us. It is the word *deilos*, which is translated as "timidity or moral cowardice."

When I think of cowardice I find myself confronting two expressions of this nasty inner experience. Undoubtedly there is physical cowardice where I shrink away from a dangerous situation such as standing on the brink of a high cliff or diving too deep and being unable to breath until I could surface. In such cases the threat is to the physical person. It is a survival mechanism I believe God endowed us with.

However for the other kind of fear, moral cowardice, I am damned with a most severe judgement.

I know well the situations where I am confronted with an encounter where my integrity or reputation is at risk. If I go to that person they will judge and condemn me. So I won't go to them. If I apply for that job my past career failures will be revealed so I won't apply. If I seek that position in the church they will see how I have sinned in the past, so I won't seek that position. Each one of these situations is moral cowardice at work. However, if I am to understand why the Lord used this strong word in His rebuke of His disciples I will have to know what else the Scriptures could teach me about this expression of the old man.

The Scriptural Record

In the Scriptures the word *deilos* was used only on five occasions. The first instance is found in Matthew, who used it in conjunction with the term "of little faith." In recounting the same event Mark used the same word, but he gave Jesus different words from those reported by Matthew. He wrote that Jesus said, "Why are you so afraid? Do you still have no faith?" (Mark 4:40). It is worth noting that both Matthew and Mark connected *deilos*, "moral cowardice," with *pistis*, "faith." One opposed to the other.

John also reported Jesus' use of this word in the upper room where He connected the experience of moral cowardice with an experience of the heart. He told His disciples, "Peace I leave with you; my peace I give you. I do not give to you as the world gives. Do not let your hearts be troubled and do not be afraid" (John 14:27). Do not be moral cowards. Let your trust in the Father stand in bold opposition to the aggression of the Jews.

Jesus' words let me see as Jesus sees into the conditions of my own heart. There revealed in all his stark nastiness is the old man of sin. Jesus' words can be paraphrased, "Don't let your heart be troubled, stirred up, agitated, like waters in a turgid pool, with various human emotions generated by the old man that replace one's peace. Also, do not let the old man cower you into moral cowardice by letting reason and emotional responses dictate your choice not to trust Jesus as Saviour and Lord."

I dare to believe that the old man, deeply versed as he is in the ways of the adversary, hates peace and will do anything to escape that paramount gift from the Father. When the old man is faced with the choice between anxiety and being filled with the Lord's peace, I discover that naturally within me, he is, I am, a moral coward. Unable to face that choice the old man usually retreats into his own kind of perverse and reverse security a troubled, disturbed, and agitated heart. Surely that is why Paul instructs us, "Put to death, therefore, whatever belongs to your earthly nature, [your old man]" (Col. 3:5).

There are two other instances of the use of this word *deilos*, translated as moral cowardice. The first is in Timothy. Paul made the matter of timidity and moral cowardice a central issue in writing to his spiritual son. He wrote, "For God did not give us a spirit of timidity [*deilos*], but a spirit of power, and of love and of self-discipline" (2 Tim. 1:7). Here the two ways stand sharply in contrast: the old man with his timidity and moral cowardice, afraid to face and make the bitter choices; and my human spirit filled to the brink with His Spirit in response to my trust.

I did not know the final reference to moral cowardice existed, but this verse has the power to shake me out of my complacency. It is found in Revelation and occurs after the Lord had promised a new heaven and a new earth where, "He will wipe every tear from their eyes. There will be no more death or mourning or crying or pain, for the old order of things has passed away" (Rev. 21:4). The disruptive voices and demands of the old man in His disciples will be stilled forever. But not quite.

The prophet then lists those whose eternal lot will be the lake of burning sulphur which is the second death. I am not surprised by some of those on the list: murderers, idolaters, liars, sexual immoral persons, and those who practice magic arts. However, the two groups of people who top the list force me to do a serious rethink of what I believe. The two groups are the moral cowards (*deilois*), and those without faith (*apistoi*).

Why should I be surprised? These are the Father's own priorities. Dare I admit to myself that they set the standard against how I will be judged for all my works, and appropriately rewarded (or chastened) at the Judgement Seat of Christ? In eternal matters these two words also set the standard against which those who are not His disciples will be judged. We will be judged with hope for our eternal reward. Those who fail the test of faith will be judged without hope, and can expect the lake of fire that burns forever. We are saved because we trust Him without reservation and place our lives unreservedly in His hands. They are doomed because they reject the Lordship of the Only Son of the Father.

Here in the words of the prophet I find a most unlikely bond between myself and those who languish eternally in the lake of fire. We have both shared the same old man. However, with me, as with all His disciples, the old man who is eternally hostile to the Father, has been crucified with Christ (Gal. 2:20) and it remains for me to daily put him to death.

There is one final challenge in this prophecy of the times of the end. It is also a promise for His disciples who face the old man and know where he belongs, in the dustbin of all God's discards. The challenge and the promise! "He who overcomes will inherit all this, and I will be his God and he will be my son" (Rev. 21:7). Overcomes all the voices, demands, insinuations, condemnations, suggestions, deceits, and desires of the old man. Share in the wonder of being a true son of the Father of Heaven and participate in the unimaginable wealth and glory of that eternal place.

Now I can return to the twelve disciples in the boat after the Lord had rebuked them for their lack of faith and their moral cowardice. What was the choice they had failed in? Let us trace through the sequence of events in that boat.

The Disciples' Choice

Jesus was tired after a whole night in prayer and a day teaching the crowd on the hillside. He reclined on a cushion in the stern and fell asleep while the disciples continued to steer the boat towards the far shore and keep a careful trim on the sail. The wind rose, the waves began to slap against the sides of the boat, and the sail and ropes began to creak with ominous sounds as they stretched towards breaking point.

The disciples knew those weather conditions very well indeed—at least the fishermen from Capernaum did—and they knew that unless something dramatic happened they would be swamped and their lives probably lost. Panic set in. However, there in the boat slept the One who had already demonstrated His power over demons, illness, and blindness. Their only choice, call Him to respond to their very urgent need. Nonetheless they refrained until panic driven anxiety took over and they cried out, "Teacher, don't you care if we drown?" (Mark 4:38). What they were saying in their extreme fear was, "we will be utterly and completely destroyed, ruined, lost, brought to nought, put to death."

My first impulse is to identify with the twelve. The Lord is asleep. We won't wake Him. Let's suffer as long as we can. Poor me! However, there was no trust in the boat, only the wilful decision not to involve the Lord until it was almost too late. Therein laid their moral cowardice. When they did finally involve Him their cry was not impelled by trust, but by the first and ultimate kind of fear, the fear of death.

When Jesus was woken by their cry He understood that their problem wasn't the fear of death, but the second kind of fear, *deilos*. They were guilty of moral cowardice because they had drawn back from calling on the Lord and the placing their lives in His capable hands. They had instead taken refuge in fearful anxiety preferring to leave their lives at the mercy of the waters that would certainly bring about their death unless they could call on the Lord and trust Him in their distress.

Their choice between the way of faith and the ways of the old man earned them the Lord's rebuke. Moral cowards, men of little faith, or as Mark reported the incident, Men of no faith (see Mark 4:40 where the KJV renders Jesus' words as, "How have you not faith?" To add the paraphrase that expresses my own heart's cry,

"Haven't you placed your implicit trust in the Son of God to intervene in your life threatening dilemma?").

Why did they collapse into the arms of moral cowardice? What prevented them from advancing into the forefront of this battle with the elements and with their own natural fear? Why indeed did the Lord put on record that they had acted as moral cowards? I know what tumbles me out of my rest into the panic, frustration, and confusion of being a moral coward, but not the disciples. The record is silent. Only Jesus' words so long ago testify that this activity of the old man had asserted itself in their responses in the boat.

Matthew and Mark record two of the activities of the old man that are evident in the lives of these disciples, anxiety which we dealt with in the first part of this chapter, and now fear, moral cowardice. I wonder if the disciples were as conscious of these inner malignancies of the old man as I am. After all I have probably had twice as many years as they had to be confronted and humbled by his depredations. However, it is wrong to think that anxiety and moral cowardice are all that the old man is capable of. He is much more devious than that.

Katie was faced with a great and terrifying darkness in her house. Her children were at school and the house, apart from herself, was empty. Yet it was both empty, and not empty. As she walked from room to room she was followed by a presence that threatened her peace, opposed her faith, and filled every room with evil. In desperation she called me at work and then went to wait outside the house. I felt the evil as soon as we entered the front door. It clutched at my throat trying to stop me speaking and calling on the Lord's name. However, acceptance of this evil wasn't an option, besides I had been praying forcefully all the way to Katie's house. I resisted the evil presence. I called on the Lord's name to rid the house of that presence and He did. In every room and passageway until the house was clean again.

Katie wasn't a moral coward. Though she could have folded up her will and crept away in defeat, she didn't. Instead she did all that she knew to do. Jesus wasn't there in person, but I was, and He was present within me. Through her faith and with the authority the Lord gives for all such occasions the angel of the adversary was sent packing. Light triumphed over darkness.

Inner Realities

As I face into the twenty first century I am confronted by an uncomfortable truth. Within my inner being two voices call for my attention. The seductive voice of the old man, and the still small voice of the Lord. It is as though I have an inner garden in my spirit where the wisest and most gracious of persons walks and talks with me. It is like a miniature garden of Eden before the adversary came. Around my garden is a stout wall where there are a number of doors that can only be unlocked from the inside. Only I have the keys to these doors.

My garden is perfect as it must be for the One who lives there. However, when I unlock any of the doors unruly outsiders thrust their way into my garden bringing with them their graffiti, rubbish, and the strident sounds of their laughter. They would stay forever if I let them.

When they come they trample over all that is perfect and beautiful in my garden. They seek to crush and destroy the living things I have so carefully tended and they cause the wise person who lives in my garden to withdraw. He will not compete with the unruly ones I have admitted. It is only when I refuse to acknowledge the right of the intruders to trample over all that is holy in my garden and so stifle the voice of the Lord within; only when I lock the doors of my heart and will against them; only when there is silence again in my garden will the Wise One reappear and bring with Him the sound of His voice and the songs He sings. Only then will His peace and tranquillity descend again over my garden and all the sacred precincts of the place where He dwells within me be filled with His love.

My garden is my heart; the Wise One is my Lord, and the unruly intruders are the voices of the old man who is opposed to all that the Lord would bring to my heart and all that He would express there. I know, as Paul knew, that the old man cannot please the Father and stands opposed to all that the Father would bring to His disciples in the twenty-first century.

This old sinful nature that loves to inhabit and run rampant around my inner garden is also opposed to all that the Lord needs to do in the world. I must stand with my Lord against the depredations of the old man as the Lord brings His people into the revival that will sweep away the dross of history. For He will prepare His own *ekklesia*, the Body of Christ, as His bride for the marriage feast of the Lamb.

There in the sanctity of my inner garden with the doors securely locked against the old man, the world, and the agents of the adversary, will the Lord reveal to me what He wants me to do for Him and with Him. In my inner garden I can be filled to the limit with all the fullness of the Father Himself, and in so being, will know the will of the Father for me in His church in the twenty-first century.

Chapter Eight

The Problem of Doubt

Thomas

He has been called "Doubting Thomas," and so the name has come down to us firmly embedded in Christian and secular thought. However, the sobriquet may not be altogether appropriate. The term "doubt" does not appear in any of the records regarding Thomas who was also called the Twin or Didymus.

Thomas is referred to in the list of the disciples in Matthew, Mark, Luke and Acts, but it is only in John that we see anything of the man. John first refers to Thomas when Jesus and the disciples were across the Jordan where John had been baptising. Jesus had received word that Lazarus was dead and that He was going to bring him back from the sleep of death. Thomas said to the group, "Let us also go, that we may die with him" (John 11:16).

At first glance this seems a strange statement, but Thomas' words have to be read in context. When Jesus said to His disciples, "Let us go back to Judea," they knew that this was most dangerous and they protested, "a short while ago the Jews tried to stone you, and yet you are going back there?" (John 11:8). Death at the hands of the Jews was high on the list of their fears and Thomas knew this. His statement, "Let us also go that we may die with Him," reveals a young man whose character is without dispute. He would go where Jesus went, even into danger, and if necessary he would die with the Master. Is this courage? Probably, though it is couched in the language of an impulsive young man.

The next reference, again in John, reveals a little more of this disciple. Jesus had told them that He was going to prepare a place for them in His Father's house where there were many rooms. He then added, "You know the way to the place where I am going" (John 14:4). Obviously Thomas had not understood that Jesus was referring to Himself as the way. Again we find the same impulsive young man whose mind had trouble keeping up with his tongue. Thomas responds, "Lord we don't know where you are going, so how can we know the way?" (John 14:5).

John's report reveals an honest young man whose whole approach to life—as we shall see—was based on fact. Thomas was concerned with what he could see. His faith rested on what could be proved. So it was when Thomas rejoined the disciples in the upper room and there heard that Jesus was alive. His response, "Unless I see the nail marks in his hands and put my fingers where the nails were, and put my hand into his side, I will not believe" (John 20:25). Thomas' words are emphatic. They can better be translated, "By no means will I believe" (literal translation in Greek).

When Jesus returned to that room through locked doors He said to them, "Peace be with you" (John 20:26). Now I find myself witnessing a most holy moment. Jesus then went to Thomas whom He knew faced a personal crisis of faith. Standing in front of Thomas He held out His hands and said, "Put your finger here; see my hands." And laying bare the wound in His side He said, "Reach out your hand and put it into my side" (John 20:27).

Jesus knew that the only way for Thomas to step into faith was for His disciple to receive this most intimate gift. His hands where Thomas knew the nails had held his Lord to the cross, and the side that had been pierced by the soldier's spear. Jesus was taking Thomas back to the cross and to the terrible truth of His crucifixion. It was there on the cross that Thomas' faith had truly been purchased.

Jesus knew that for Thomas what he could see, feel, and touch was the basis of his faith and discipleship. So the Lord met His disciple at the only place where that disciple could make a new beginning. At the place where Thomas stumbled because of his need for undisputed facts, He gave His disciple the one fact that had been missing from Thomas' understanding. The fact of His own body. The fact of the crucifixion of His body made personal for His disciple. The Lord added to that fact by displaying the wounds in His hands and side, which show the inescapable fact of His life from the dead. For He was indeed alive in that upper room.

Thomas understood. He let his heart and mind take these formidable facts into his own being. I imagine him falling at the feet of His Saviour and Lord and crying out, "My Lord and my God!" (John 20:28).

There were six more words in Jesus' statement to Thomas that I have passed over but which we must now examine. These words add the crucial ingredient to that intimate transaction. Jesus' words to Thomas are, "and be not faithless, but believing" (John 20:27, KJV).

Before we consider these words I have to ask you to bear with some Greek vocabulary. There are three Greek words normally translated as "doubt." The first can be translated, "to be in strife with one's self hence to hesitate and waver." The second means, "to stand in two ways and to be undecided which way to take." The third means, "to be without resource, to know not what to do."

Jesus did not use any of these doubt words when He spoke with Thomas. Instead He used two forms of the same word, one negative—*apistos*; one positive—*pistos*. Thomas would have understood the sense of what Jesus was saying to him, "Don't be a disciple who is *apistos*, not worthy of the Lord's confidence, untrustworthy, faithless, the kind of person who refuses to receive the Lord's revelation of grace. Instead be a disciple who is *pistos*, faithful, trustworthy, worthy of confidence, sure, firm, certain, and believing."

So I stand with Thomas and heed the Lord's words, for He intends that what He said to Thomas be imprinted on the hearts and minds of all those who would be His disciples in the twenty-first century. I find myself wanting to tell Him I understand my need to commit myself to be faithful and believing. Then I want to bow at the feet of the Crucified One and affirm that He is my Lord and my God. I want to entreat Him to teach me what is needed in my life so that He can trust me with the terrible gift of His own body hanging there between heaven and earth and now, in spirit, dwelling within me. I want Him to trust me like Thomas with the wounds in His hands and side, and the eternal facts of His life and death and living again. I believe that only so, can I truly be His disciple.

Peter

Some of the inescapable facts in the life of any of Jesus' disciples are the highs and lows of faith. At times we feel as though we have fulfilled Isaiah's familiar words, "They shall mount up with wings as eagles; they shall run, and not be weary; and they shall walk, and not faint" (Isa. 40:31). However, at other times the very opposite overtakes us. We find ourselves grounded with our feet fastened securely in muddy clay and unable to place one foot in front of another. We wonder why the peace disappeared into pain and where the song went in the grey hours when the Lord seems like a far distant friend.

These experiences in faith are part of a continuum. We move out of the lofty place where we fly, into the grey fog of unknowing, and then, by His grace, back again. It is a mistake to fasten our attention on either the open skies or the muddy surrounds for our feet as though they could not be connected. They are certainly connected, but faith links these separate and opposite experiences together with the One who understands them both. So it was for Peter.

In this part of our study into the obstacles of faith we begin with Peter's commissioning with the other eleven disciples when Jesus sent them out with, "authority to drive out evil spirits and to heal every disease and sickness" (Matt. 10:1). His instructions, "As you go preach this message, 'The kingdom of heaven is near.' Heal the sick, raise the dead, cleanse those who have leprosy, drive out demons."

Peter knew what it meant for his faith to fly. He had been sent out under the Lord's authority into the towns of Galilee as one of His twelve apostles and everything the Lord instructed them to do was brought into being. Mark reported that

"They went out and preached that people should repent. They drove out many demons and anointed many sick people with oil and healed them" (Mark 6:12, 13).

Following their return Peter witnessed the Lord's power at work; healing the man with a shrivelled hand (Matt. 12:9–13), healing the sick (Matt. 12:15), and healing the demon possessed man who was blind and mute (Matt. 12:22). The final miracle that continued to impress Peter's mind and heart with the power, compassion, and authority of his Lord was the feeding of the five thousand. If I had been there in those days, my faith, like Peter's, would have flown on eagle's wings and I would have felt that I could run forever and never be weary and walk this path of faith with my indomitable Lord until the sun sets on the path forever. However, then the stumble came for Peter. He fell out of the high glory of faith into the pit of fear.

After Jesus had dismissed the crowd when they had been fed, He went up a nearby mountain alone to pray while the disciples set out in one of their boats for the other side of the lake. When they were some distance from the shore the wind rose against them and Jesus appeared to them walking on the waters. They were afraid because they thought they were seeing a ghost (Matt. 14:26). He responded to their fear. "Take courage! It is I. Don't be afraid" (Matt. 14:27).

Peter wasn't troubled by the turbulence of the waves. His fear could only have been a minor interruption in his faith. Now he could see that the Lord had power even over the laws of nature that would have sunk an ordinary man. He would have added this to the long list of wonders he had witnessed at the Lord's hand and that he himself had participated in. This was only one more experience when his faith would have flown higher than the mountains. In that exalted glory he cried out to the Lord, "Lord, if it's you, tell me to come to you on the water" (Matt. 14:28). The Lord, seeing Peter's faith, replied without hesitation, "Come" (Matt. 14:29). So his faith yielded its fruit, but only for such a short time and then it was over. He saw the waves and being afraid began to sink. Peter would have continued downward to a dark grave had not the Lord reached out His hand and caught him.

It wasn't only Peter's body that was under threat that day. It was also his faith. Jesus' gentle rebuke tells its own story. "You of little faith, why did you doubt?" (Matt. 14:31). The high soaring eagle had had its wings clipped. The exaltation of those previous days had been eclipsed and so Peter's faith had to give way to this other obstacle of faith. It was doubt.

However, there was more to Peter's descent out of the realm of faith. Fear had introduced—or more likely, re-introduced—him to the deceits of the old man. Fear at first because he thought he was seeing a ghost, and then fear because he saw the wind, literally the effect the wind had on the waters of the lake. Fear opened the door and doubt quickly entered the place where trust in the Lord should have kept this disciple at rest.

Doubt split Peter's mind in two. Two ways. Two paths for his feet. It was either the way of faith on top of the waters in victory over the circumstances, which his faith would have conquered, or the way of doubt trapping his feet in the circumstances that were against him, dragging him down to what would have been a watery death. The same dilemma confronts all of Jesus' disciples. Do we focus on the circumstances and become confused by the path that we should take or focus on the Lord and trust Him and feel His hands lift us out of situations, ideas, relationships, or words that would drag us under? Live in doubt, and faith dies. Live in faith, and doubt has no occasion that it can anchor its energies on. Try and live with both doubt and faith, and faith by default will always be the casualty.

James

There would have been a great deal of discussion in the house of Mary and Joseph in Nazareth. The half-brother of James, Joseph, Simon, and Judas had left the family business for the life of a wandering rabbi. They would have heard all the reports from the place across the Jordan where Jesus had been baptised by that other wandering teacher, John, a relative of theirs through Mary's family. There would have also been disturbing reports about casting out demons, and healing the blind, lepers, and cripples. Reports from Samaria, Judea, and the holy city itself, turned everything they had known about their half-brother on its head.

It was no wonder that some people said that He was beside Himself. The word means, "to change from one condition, that of the stay at home half brother, to another person entirely, to be driven out of his senses." Was this the person who was skilled in the tools of His trade? The one who was so filled with wisdom and compassion? It would not have been surprising if James, the eldest of Mary and Joseph's sons, had entertained doubt about Jesus.

James would have known what it meant for him not to believe in the Son of God. He would have resisted the path of faith that the twelve disciples had chosen, but whether because of initial doubt about Jesus or because of pressures from the Jews who wanted to kill Him we cannot know (see John 7:1). All we have is John's report, "For even his own brothers did not believe in him" (John 7:5). James and his three brothers did not give Jesus their unreserved and unconditional trust with the surrender of their lives to His Lordship.

We don't know when James became one of the Lord's disciples, but Paul reports that after His resurrection Jesus was seen by Peter (Cephas) then by the twelve (we infer that the twelve included Mattaias since Judas had been excluded, see

Acts 1:24–26). Then Jesus was seen by five hundred disciples and after that, and before His ascension, by James, His own half-brother (see 1 Cor. 15:4–7).

Did this encounter with Jesus give James the impetus to become Jesus' disciple? We can never know, but after Jesus had ascended and the Spirit had come at Pentecost, we find that James had indeed become part of that first *ekklesia* (see Acts 12:27; Gal. 1:9).

From familiarity with his own brother, to doubt, and then to faith. This was the path James had walked; from having the same earthly mother, Mary, to becoming a son of the eternal Father and Jesus' true brother in the Spirit. So many of us, if we are honest with ourselves and with the Lord, will readily identify with these experiences. I know all about the familiarity that organised religion breeds. Doubt is no stranger in my human relationships and discipleship. However, above and beyond the undemanding smoke screen of institutional religion there is faith in the living Son of God. So I come back once again to the subject of my inquiry.

Around thirty years after Pentecost James was still in Jerusalem where he wrote the letter that bears his name. I am not surprised to find in the first chapter of that letter references to both faith and doubt. James knew a lot about both of these emotions.

When Jesus rebuked Peter when He held him as he began to sink beneath the waves he used the word *distazo*, which is translated doubt. It means, "to stand in two ways and to be uncertain which of the two ways to take." James picked up the same theme when he counselled those who need to ask the Father for wisdom. He wrote, "But when [the disciple] asks, he must believe and not doubt." The word James used, and which is also translated "doubt" means, "to contend, to be in strife with one's self, to hesitate, to waver." Also, James added the compelling description of those who let doubt stand in the way of faith. "He who doubts is like a wave of the sea, blown and tossed by the wind" (James 1:6).

I have to be the first to acknowledge that doubt is a very subtle foe hiding its voice in the many reasonable arguments I use to excuse my lack of power, prayers that were never answered, difficulties in relationships that could not be resolved, or resources I needed but could not access. "It's not a question of my faith," I tell myself. "The circumstances were sent to try me. The enemy is at the gates. It was never meant to be." I could go on forever. "It's not the Lord's will." You know them all.

Behind all these reasonable arguments is the failure of my trust. He does not have my heart. I have reserved it for myself so that I don't have to surrender all of myself to Him as my Lord. In that surrender, I don't have to trust Him without question.

In all these specious arguments, doubt is well hidden. I can keep it so well hidden that I can pretend to myself that my faith and discipleship are intact. However, when I step away from argument and face inward where the Lord dwells and the Spirit brings "all truth," I have to acknowledge that these failures of faith are not because of some "out there" factors. The failure is within. If I open my heart to His voice I will find within myself the two ways the Lord spoke about to Peter when He caught him above the waves. I also find there in that inner secret place my own inability to face the truth that James described.

It is an unfortunate fact of life that I can so easily skate on life's surface. I can attend all the church services, read my Bible diligently, go to all the prayer meetings, and yet never face inward. I did that for so many years and was seemingly content. Never listen to the voice of the Spirit revealing my own truth to me. Refuse to acknowledge that my trust is Him is faulty. Argue my own way out of failure. Listen to any other voice than His voice within. I have done all that. However, when I allow the Spirit to overcome the obstacles I put in His path I am forced to acknowledge the two ways, the division of my mind and heart as I contend with myself against myself. I find doubt.

James had another word for this obstacle to faith. He called it being double minded or having two souls. One soul is the old man. The other is the renewed spirit (see James 1:6–8; 2 Cor. 5:17). The old unredeemable part of me, the old man, knows all about doubt. It is like the air he breathes. The other part of me, my born again spirit where the Holy Spirit breathes His own life, can rise on eagles' wings in unconquerable trust in my Lord. The question is, which of the two will I heed as I face into the twenty-first century? Doubt and unconquerable trust or the faith that prevails? Which will I heed?

Chapter Nine

Conformed to the Image of Christ

Why Do I Believe?

There are many questions we ask as we move forward in the faith. When we face a vexing situation that disturbs our ordered lifestyle: Why is He putting me through this? When something heartbreaking overtakes us like the loss of a wife or child: Why did He let this happen? When a desperate prayer for someone in need isn't answered: Why doesn't He answer? On a larger scale; Why does He allow so many to suffer from famine and pestilence and genocide? There are no answers from the Most High.

Like so many others I have had to learn the uncomfortable truth that God rarely answers questions that begin with "why." However, there is one "why" question He has answered. It is the question, Why am I here? To put the question in the terms of my own search; Why do I believe? What is the Father's answer to my question? Because He predestined me to conformed to the image of His Son (Rom. 8:29).

Image; *eikonos*, refers not merely to the visual and outer image, but to the pattern in the original, which portrays the likeness intended to be found in the image. Image and pattern, but pattern came first. Image followed. For, "God created man in His own image, in the image of God He created him" (Gen. 1:27). The pattern in the Father. The image in His created being.

Predestine: *proorizo*, to set bounds before, to determine, decree, or ordain beforehand. "*Proorizo* precedes history. Those who in history God foreknows are the subjects of what He has before all history prepared and counselled for them" (Bullinger, *A Critical Lexicon and Concordance* [Bagster, London, 1974]).

The term translated "predestine" only occurs four times in the New Testament. In each case the writer is Paul, and in each case he refers to the purpose of the Father concerning His children.

In his letter to the Ephesian assembly Paul wrote, "He predestined us to be adopted as his sons through Jesus Christ, in accordance with his pleasure and will" (Eph. 1:5), and, "In him we were also chosen, having been predestined according to the plan of him who works out everything in conformity with the purpose of his will" (Eph. 1:11).

The word also occurs twice in his letter to the Roman assembly. Paul wrote, "For those God foreknew, he also predestined to be conformed to the likeness [image] of his Son, that he might be the firstborn among many brothers. And those he predestined he also called" (Rom. 8:29, 30).

Predestined according to the purposes of the Father. Known across the panoply of time. Predestined before history to be adopted as sons, to be chosen, to be called into His family, to be transformed into the image of His Son. Mine was not some sort of accidental conversion when I chanced to hear the words of the gospel, and certainly not a purpose that requires the agreement of the institutional church. Nor does it refer to God's response to a random attack of guilt because of something I have done. Being predestined is supremely intentional. Planned. Filled with the Father's purpose. All this before the order went out to create man in the image of God.

The Spirit who inspired these words lets me see for a brief instant into the mind of the Father Himself. He knew me and predestined me to be conformed to the image of His eternal Son. That was before history began to scribble its indelible lines across the pages of mankind. Also, this is what the Father intended for all who would believe, before Adam was created, before sin overtook the world, before Christ was born. Then He had all of us in mind for we are integral parts of the Father's purposes for the world and for mankind.

I like to think that history is not merely a straight line catalogue of man's achievements and mistakes. That is man's view. God's view I believe is different. History is not linear, but cyclical. When I read of Eve's temptation and the sin of the first couple I am tempted to think that that part of man's history is over. His purposes were blighted by the adversary and His creative acts in the garden would never to be repeated. I believe that the purposes of the Father are as eternal as He is eternal. The Father's purposes once declared and set in motion are never terminated until the purpose of those initiatives has been achieved.

Being conformed to the image of the Father and of His Son can be told in four acts, for this is a cyclic drama of God's intentional purpose. The first was enacted long ago when mankind was almost still born. The second and third acts were depicted for us when Rome ruled the world. The final act has yet to take place.

Act One: Adam Created in the Image of God

The pattern the Father used to make man was Himself. Not simply His capacities for moral judgement, reflective thought, the exercise of will, ability to relate to another, or His creative energies. These can be thought of merely as static doctrines, like looking at the glass of a window on which these two dimensional patterns have been etched. Of course the patterns the Father used in the creation of Adam were not like images on a flat photograph. Each image involved the throb of divine life, the Father's own infinite and eternal life in all its complex beauty and wonder.

All the Father's capacities were etched into Adam's being when he was created from the red dust of the earth. His body came from the earth. His life came from God who, "breathed into his nostrils the breath of life, and the man became a living being" (Gen. 2:7). I do not believe—and there is nothing in the Scriptures to suggest—that the Father bestowed only part of His divine nature on Adam. In God the pattern was complete and in Adam the image was perfect. For God had created Adam in the complete image of Himself. Adam became alive with the life and spirit of God Himself, truly made in the image of the Father, from the inside out; nothing missed; nothing lacking.

Just as God was love itself, so Adam was love. As God was eternally at peace and filled with His own peace, so Adam was filled with this expression of his Father's own character. Also, as the Father was the centre of the great songs of worship that filled the universe that were sung by the vast angelic choirs, so Adam had been created to fill the garden in Eden with songs of joy rising out of the inner beauty of his own spirit. The Scriptures don't tell me this is so, but how could it not be?

However, there is more. Adam was instructed to, "Be fruitful and increase in numbers; fill the earth and subdue it. Rule over the fish of the sea and the birds of the air and over every living creature that moves on the ground" (Gen. 1:28). I believe that the Father made man in the image of Himself so that the whole earth could be filled with the Father's own love and so that His peace could provide the eternal covering of divinity within man and for man. I believe that the Father intended that the whole earth would be filled with praise, worship, songs of joy, and that God Himself could continue to walk among and be present with His people.

I believe that Adam was made in the Father's image so that all the relationships between all of his descendants could be marked with compassion, understanding, equity, and justice. Friendship would be unparalleled. The gift of one person to another would be without cost or demand. Mankind would be without conflict. The earth would yield her bounty without stint and famine. Pestilence would be unknown.

Man was made in the image of God so that he with God could rule the earth and all that God had created, including himself (see Gen. 1:28). Instead the adversary substituted his own evil rule for the righteous rule of the man that God had created. One might say that the Father's purposes had been frustrated. But this is not so! The Father would repeat that creative act, making man in His own image, until the purposes of God in creation were complete. The image reproduced in the first man had indeed been made after the pattern of the Father; and then sin intruded and almost everything was lost. Act Two follows Act One as surely as the day follows the sunrise.

Act Two: Christ Came in the Image of the Father

In order for man to regain the image of God that was lost in the garden the Father had to send another to undo that damage. Also, because of the sinful nature Adam had brought with him out of the garden he failed in his commission to people the world with offspring filled with grace, love, compassion, justice, and mercy. God had to send another so that Adam's sinful nature could be put in its place. Paul wrote, "For what the law was powerless to do in that it was weakened by the sinful nature [inherited from Adam], God did by sending his Son in the likeness of sinful man to be a sin offering" (Rom. 8:3).

The first image of the Father in man had failed because of the adversary's deceit so a second Person, also like Adam exhibiting the image of God, had to be sent among men so that the prior damage in Adam could be undone. Paul wrote that, "The Son [Jesus] is the image of the invisible God, the firstborn over all creation" (Col. 1:15). The same word; *eikonos*, is used. The Son is the complete image of the Father. Jesus told His disciples, "Anyone who has seen me has seen the Father" (John 14:9). This shows the pattern and image. The pattern in the Father. The image in the Son. The image was a complete expression of the Father on the streets of Jerusalem as well as the roads of Judea, Samaria, and Galilee.

Jesus said, "Peace I leave with you; my peace I give you" (John 14:27). Jesus' peace was the Father's own peace for Paul wrote of "the peace of God, which transcends all understanding" (Phil. 4:7). Also, love! Jesus told His disciples, "As the Father has loved me, so have I loved you" (John 15:9). There is pattern, image, and joy also! Paul wrote, "May the God of hope fill you will all joy" (Rom. 15:13). The Father is the pattern and the source of joy, and this joy filled my Lord. He told His disciples, "I have told you this so that my joy may be in you" (John 15:11). My joy! Need more be said?

We see the image of the Father in all that Jesus did and said. However, there is one further statement of pattern and image in the Father and the Son. It is found in the other person of the Godhead; the Spirit of Truth, for He also expresses the eternal life of the Father and Son. Paul taught the disciples in the assemblies in Galatia regarding the fruit of the Spirit and used the word "fruit" to express the person and character of the Spirit. He went on to list elements of the character of the Spirit of God that I believe are also elements of the character of our Lord. "Love, joy, peace, patience, kindness, goodness, faithfulness, gentleness, self control" (Gal. 5:22). The elements of character exist in the Son and are expressed by the Spirit because they are found in the pattern who is the Father.

Then Jesus, made after the pattern of the Father's own life, "humbled himself and took on Himself the form of a servant and became obedient unto death, even the death of the cross" (Phil. 2:8). In those agonising moments when all His sinews were stretched against the nails, He completed the first stage of the process that would purchase my salvation, undo the terrible heritage out of Eden when the first image of God in man was corrupted, and make it possible for the Father to set in motion the next act of creating man in His own image. However, first He had to rise again and complete the work of my redemption and then ascend to the Father.

Act Three: Inner Transformation Into the Image of Christ

The Father's own words; "For whom he did foreknow, he also did predestinate to be conformed to the image of his Son" (Rom. 8:29, KJV). Pattern and image. The pattern in the Son who lives within me (see Gal. 2:20) and the image is recreated within every disciple who walks in trust with the Son. Now I have to stand on this very high place of revelation and challenge my mind to grasp the incomprehensible. It is Jesus within me. This is my heritage. For this reason I have been predestined; not simply to receive and to enter salvation; not simply to receive forgiveness and the wonder of heaven; not merely to be chosen of God and enrolled in the annals of the throne room; and not merely to be called a child of the Father. The Father stated through His Spirit that I have been predestined to be conformed to that everlasting image of His eternal Son.

I find myself in awe of this God I worship, for in that fateful moment when Eve and then Adam tasted the forbidden fruit, the Father knew who I was (see Jer. 1:5; Eph. 1:4). I also was present in the Father's mind and heart before the world was brought into being and certainly I was known when Eve and Adam turned the Father's purpose on its head. Now as we approach the end of the age I know I am also called to be part of that same eternal purpose, to be conformed to the image of His eternal Son.

The word for conformed in Greek is *summorphos*, which means to have a like form with another person. Jesus is that other person. He is love. So He intends that I also be love. He is peace. So I must allow Him to fill me with His peace. He is joy. So must that inexpressible element of His personality be found in me. He is compassion. The grace of that infinite pity must be expressed in all my relationships, as it was in His. He has come to do the will of the Father. So must I. He was crucified. I, in my walk with Him, while never knowing the pain of the nails, must be always willing for the death of the old man as I have been crucified with Christ (see Gal. 2:20).

The Father has predestined me to be conformed in all my being to the image of His Son. Nothing should be left out. This is not a partial transformation. I cannot choose the elements of His person I want to have expressed within myself, and those I would like left on the shelf of my selfishness. Nor is it a partial transformation by default, because my lack of knowledge and understanding of these things damns me to walk in partial fulfilment of the Father's purposes. I am to be transformed into the complete image of my Lord; the inexpressibly wonderful and powerful love and grace filled image of the Son (see John 1:14).

I have one thing to add in this search and it comes in the form of a confession. All my attempts to reproduce those, "fruits of the Spirit," to have those elements of His character permanently present in my own life, have failed. I do not have the strength, capacity, or the wisdom to transform myself. I have to be transformed by another, and that One is the Spirit of the Father and of Christ (see 2 Cor. 3:18).

The Pattern

There are some obnoxious myths abroad in the Christian church. One is that all Christians need to do is to live after His example. This teaching tells us to discover the patterns expressed in His life and then try and bring these patterns to life without any recourse to His spirit and power. I have no difficulty believing that we are meant to live as He lived, for He said that His disciples would do greater things than what their Lord had done (see John 14:12). However, a life that strips His example of His power is fruitless and powerless no matter how hard we try.

A second myth is that all we need to do is to fasten our attention on the truths that the Scriptures reveal. According to this partial truth the patterns for my transformation into the image of my Lord are spelled out in Scripture. Believe that they are true and that is enough. Understand what the Scriptures teach. Fasten my mind around those truths. Be prepared to argue and preach them when I have opportunity, and that is sufficient. Such Christians, like many in Christendom, ignore the fact that the sources of the patterns for my transformation are to be found in the living Son of the Father.

Many Christians are like a person who feels he doesn't need to live in a castle filled with the glories of the universe. He has all the architect's drawings and believes that they are sufficient.

However, where exactly is the pattern for my transformation into the image of Christ? He Himself is the pattern. Where do I find these patterns? Where is His love and peace? The way He thinks? His wisdom? His compassion? His creative energies? His authority? His joy? His grace? His forgiveness? To answer my own questions I need to go back to a beginning.

When I first responded to the Lord I could never have guessed these extraordinary dimensions of my faith. It all seemed so simple, as I am sure it is for so many who follow the Lord. However, soon the puzzles began to appear. I found questions about elements hinted at in the Scriptures and how they related to my life as His disciple. I also found one of those mysteries related to the Lord Himself and His relationship with me.

I discovered that Paul called my relationship with the Master a glorious mystery, "which is Christ in you, the hope of glory" (Col. 1:27, KJV). The word translated mystery is *musterion*; the secret of a friend to be revealed to another person when the friend chooses. The Father will reveal His Son Jesus as He lives His life within me. This is the mystery that confounds me. Does this refer to the living Son of the Father, whose words brought the far flung reaches of countless galaxies into being, who was born of a virgin, who healed the lame, the blind and the leprous, who bore the agonies of crucifixion, who is beyond and before time, and who cast aside the chains of death? Does this mean the unimaginable, that the living Son of the Father will actually unveil His character within my spirit? That He will express His own life within my being? A person within a person? Yes it does! The Scriptures are clear.

The message is unequivocal. This single verse (Col. 1:27) does not stand alone. Paul affirmed the principle when he wrote, "I have been crucified with Christ and I no longer live, but Christ lives in me" (Gal. 2:20). Also, John after a lifetime of being transformed into the image of his Lord wrote, "Those who obey his commands live in him and he in them. And this is how we know that he lives in us: We know it by the Spirit he gave us" (1 John 3:24).

What better authority for this mystery than the Lord Himself. Regarding the Holy Spirit He told His disciples, "The world cannot accept him because it neither sees him nor knows him. But you know him for he lives with you and shall be in you" (John 14:17). He also spoke concerning Himself, "On that day you will realize that I am in my Father, and you are in me, and I am in you" (John 14:20).

Words from the Holy Spirit reach into corners of my brain and lodge there, but words describing the pattern for my transformation cannot themselves transform me. Only the Spirit of Christ can do that. My challenge is to discover how I can cooperate with that eternal Spirit as He undoes the tragedies of Eden and progressively transforms me into the image of my Lord.

The Process of Change

Unfortunately there are no formulas in the Scriptures that describe how the Holy Spirit changes me into the image of the Lord. No special recipes. No packaged tours the disciple can enrol in, and when it is done say, "Look I have been transformed into the image of Jesus." There is nothing like that. Looking back through the tangled web of my own life I find I am like a man who has been told of a great field of diamonds buried in the earth. I can tell you the size and colour of those precious stones and even the number of carats to the tonne. I can tell you exactly where they are and I know that they will enrich me beyond anything I can imagine, but I have a singular problem. I don't know how to bring them to the surface for they are buried under a great mass of debris and rubbish that resist any attempt I might make to get rid of it.

One demanding passage in the Scriptures calls for my undivided attention. Paul wrote; "Therefore, I urge you, brothers, in view of God's mercy, to offer your bodies as living sacrifices, holy and pleasing to God—this is your spiritual act of worship. Do not conform any longer to the pattern of this world, but be transformed by the renewing of your mind. Then you will be able to test and approve what God's will is—his good, pleasing and perfect will" (Rom. 12:1, 2). At the heart of this passage are the words, "be transformed," and Paul reminds me that this is the will of God. The good, pleasing, and perfect will of God that was first fulfilled in Eden and then lost until Christ came so that His will might be done on this earth.

Throughout this passage, I am confronted with two challenges with a caution embedded in between them. The first challenge, bring myself as a living sacrifice to the Lord. The caution, understand and find a way past the principles and concepts of the world, which, like the rubbish covering my imagined diamond field, are designed by the adversary to frustrate the process of change. The second challenge, cooperate with the Lord in the renewal of my mind.

I willingly admit that I am a novice in finding how the life of my eternal Lord can be unveiled within me so that He can express Himself in my own heart. Bringing myself as a living sacrifice has not always been understood. Nor have the ways I have been—and probably still am—conformed to this world. Also, I have not been able to connect the process of renewing my mind with things I have thought or done. I have to trust that only the Spirit of truth can embed these living truths in my mind and spirit, and show me how they must be expressed in daily living.

The First Challenge: Present Your Bodies a Living Sacrifice

Sacrifice, *thusia*, referring to the animal or person being sacrificed as well as the act of taking the life of the sacrifice. Sacrifices have no rights. They are there at the command of the Father and are intended to bridge the gap between the justice of God and His mercy.

The sacrifice of my soul is no different from the ancient sacrifices offered in the temple of Jerusalem. Placing myself on that altar is my act of worship. When I do I acknowledge His Lordship and place my life in His hands whether He wields the knife or not. This is not a single definitive act as though I could do it once and thereafter be spared the pain. This is a process. I present myself daily and in so doing make myself available for Him to transform me daily into His image.

The sacrifice has no agenda for its own life. Like the lambs for sacrifice in the temple of Jerusalem they have to be purchased just as I have been, and once purchased their only end is to die (see 1 Cor. 6:19, 20). That is the prelude to my transformation. I must set aside any rights I think I might have and place myself completely at His disposal. I must put all my agendas on the permanent back burner and present myself to Him as His sacrifice so that He might transform me into His own image.

The Caution: Be Not Conformed to the World

The word "world," *aion*, translates to age. However, it originally meant a life that was breathed away, leaving the content of the lives of men and how they live their lives.

Conformed, *suschematizo*, to form or shape myself to the form of another. I am the one carrying out this action unlike the injunction to be conformed to the image of Christ where a different word is used. In the action referred to by this word I do the forming. I am wholly responsible. In the normal course of life I shape myself to the principles of this age, rarely consciously, but the end product is that the principles of this age have been learned and entrenched in my mind, and therefore have to be unlearned. Hence Paul's words, "by the renewing of your mind."

Paul warned the disciples about the principles of the world. He wrote that they should beware, "Lest there be anyone robbing you through philosophy and empty deceit according to the traditions of men, according to the elements [basic principles] of the world, and not according to Christ" (Col. 2:8, literal translation in Greek). These are the principles that Paul understood to be opposed to the walk of faith.

The question I had to ask was, "What hinders me from being conformed to the image of His Son who lives within me?" The answer came to me as, "All the garbage I have heaped up in my mind, the traditions of men; philosophies that promise everything but deliver nothing of eternal worth; teachings and ideas that comply with and reflect the patterns of this world and have nothing to do with the life of my Lord."

The other question I had to ask was, "Why do I need to heed Paul's instructions about not being conformed to these ideas and principles of the world?" I have learned through painful and repeated experiences that my mind has to be integrally involved in this process of transformation. I cannot attend to the principles of the world and at the same time give my undivided attention to the principles of faith. Daily I have to make this choice as the world seeks to invade this sacred place where Jesus lives within me.

My natural inclinations are like familiar friends, but are so contrary to this way of the Lord. I keep telling myself that it is normal to seek and savour all the delights that the world offers. I want to have my own place in the sun. I will pursue my own dreams, however valid, and let my desires frame my future. I will open myself to all that this world has to offer. Or perhaps I am guilty of doing just that without thinking.

I have to acknowledge however, sometimes reluctantly, that the cost of being His disciple is more demanding than the easy acceptance the world would ask of its disciples. The broad way filled with all the sensual gratifications that the world promises and so readily provides, or the narrow way where my daily delights must be in the Lord alone (see Matt, 7:13, 14; 1 John 2:16). My choices are to follow Him closely and forbid an entrance to the principles of the world, or follow Him at a distance because my mind has been filled with the principles of this world.

Therefore, what response does the Lord ask me to make to the principles of the world's systems that have been lodged in my mind? I must make a response if I am to allow Him to transform me into His image. Up against my question I find a little cluster of answers. Learn to tell the difference between the principles of the world and the principles of the kingdom. Find out which of the world's principles are truly contrary to the life of faith and spirit. Discover how those principles are expressed in behaviour; in the activities of my body, mind, and heart. Find out which of the principles of the world govern my relationships. Then learn to walk away from them all; unlearn them; replace them with principles I learn as His Spirit, using the Scriptures leads me into truth.

The Second Challenge: Be Transformed by the Renewing of Your Mind

The Scriptures and the Spirit who interprets them to me, have an uncanny ability to surprise me. I find it very comfortable to think of my faith in terms of life's everyday concerns: fuel for the car, money in the bank, the job I will go to today, the concerns of this person, and the problems of that family. It is as though I never lift my eyes above my boot straps and the muddy ground around my feet. Then I encounter the words "be transformed" and decide I had better check their meaning and find out how they apply to my faith and why I believe.

The word is *metamorphoomai*, and it has been used in two places: one is used to mean touching the earth and the path I was walking, and the other reaching out of the portals of heaven. It is one word that has two applications that are related. It means, "to change one's form or appearance, to alter one's form, to transform who one is." That is what the renewing of my mind by the Spirit of truth will produce in me if I let Him.

The word is also translated "transfigured," and now it seems as if the Lord is taking me up to the summit of a very high mountain where He lets me see what His Spirit will truly do when I open myself to the renewal of my mind. This is the word Matthew used to describe what took place when, "He was transfigured before them" (Matt. 17:2, KJV). This is the same word. Just as His whole appearance was transfigured, so my spirit within me will be transfigured by the renewing of my mind.

I need to step away from that moment of transfiguration for I am afraid I might seem to bring what happened on that holy mountain down to my level and bury it in the muddy affairs of my life on earth. Rather must I ascend, step away from the mundane and ordinary, and see how the Father views the renewing of my mind. Step by painful step, each time I renounce one of the world's principles and allow the Spirit to bring new principles to birth, I believe He will transfigure my spirit. Perhaps this teaches me that my spirit will shine with the glory of the Father just as the Saviour's face shone on the mountain with that same eternal glory. That I cannot know, but Paul does make a small addition to my understanding. He wrote, "But we all, with open face beholding as in a glass the glory of the Lord, are changed into the same image from glory to glory, even as by the Spirit of the Lord" (2 Cor. 3:18, KJV).

Now we will come back to basics. I must come down from the mountain and attend to how I place my feet on the pathway. How do I attend to the renewing of my mind? The Greek word is *anakainosis*, which means, "renewal, renovation, making one's mind different from what it had been before." The words I have to lock in my understanding are, "different from what it had been before."

In the renewing of my mind I have to attend to two things. The first is what has been stored away in my mind: the concepts, principles, knowledge, wisdom, ideas, both good and bad, which are locked away in the neural networks of my brain. The second is to occupy myself with mature reflection, to let my mind make the proper connections, to reason, consider, conclude. I am challenged to discover how what I know, as well as how I think and reflect can be renewed. Paul had something to say about both these renovations of the mind.

I have to confess that for so many years I had neither the wit nor the sense to question what I had stored away in the networks of my brain. If you had asked me what came from the Spirit and what came from the systems of the world, I would have had difficulty explaining the difference. I had probably, without thinking, simply treated the principles of the kingdom as some kind of spiritual overlay, over the principles of the world that I had been quietly and unconsciously assimilating since childhood. It is only now as I give my careful attention to what the Scriptures teach and what the Spirit with His still small voice whispers into my heart and mind, that I have become aware of the distinction.

Paul instructed the disciples at Philippi, "Let this mind be in you which was also in Christ Jesus" (Phil. 2:5, KJV). I believe this instruction to me can be paraphrased, "Let the principles that governed the life of my Lord also govern my own life. Store them away in my head so that they act like lights to expose the dark and smudged principles, concepts and ideas I have borrowed from the world."

In that same passage Paul gives me three of the attitudes that governed the life of our Lord. "He took on Himself the form of a servant," servant of the Father and servant of those He came to save. "He humbled Himself," not seeking a reputation from the world of men and leaving behind anything He could have claimed as His by right. Also, "He became obedient to death," and behind that submission to the cross was His obedience to all the commands and instructions of the Father.

The standards are high indeed, but if I am to be conformed to the image of Christ then I must let these principles of obedient discipleship fill my mind and replace the dysfunctional principles that come from the world, obscuring what it means to follow Him. I must do all this while trusting my Lord with all my heart and mind.

The second part of the renewal of my mind has to do with what I think about and reflect on. Paul made a list of these things. They are all positive, but behind each one is its nasty and unprofitable counterpart. Paul gave the same instruction to the disciples at Philippi, "Whatever is true, whatever is noble, whatever is right, whatever is pure, whatever is lovely, whatever is admirable—if anything is excellent or praiseworthy—think about such things" (Phil. 4:8). Behind each of these subjects for my reflection are their ugly counterparts. I am chastened to consider how easy it has been—and in some cases still is—to give my mind over to things that are untrue, ignoble, wrong, impure, ugly, detestable, and that cannot be praised.

Now the reason for the renewal of my mind becomes clear. I am convinced that Jesus' mind could never have let such ideas penetrate His peace. He would have been fully occupied with all the attitudes in Paul's first list. So must I. My choice is to learn the qualities of what I think about, of the ideas and images I entertain, and choose those ideas that will permit His Spirit to conform me to His image. Forbid the rest.

I have one final challenge to conquer. If I am to be conformed to the image of our blessed Saviour then I must go beyond doctrine—though of course doctrine is essential—to the person of Jesus Himself. I must fill my mind with who He is, what He did, where He went, who He met, how He faced and overcame every challenge, how He related to different kinds of people, and how He expressed the eternal life of the Father among men. The life He lived in Israel is the same eternal life that He now fills my new born spirit with. In the study of His person living among men I know I will find the image of Jesus to which I long to be confirmed. The study of Jesus my Saviour must become my preoccupation.

The Final Act: Outer Transformation to the Image of the Son

There is one final act in this eternal drama. The cycle of history was not completed when Jesus rose from the dead and ascended to the Father. When I see Him, I will fully be changed. In that moment of time, the final transformation into the image of His Son will take place. John, who I believe knew a great deal about being conformed to the image of the Son, wrote, "Dear friends, now we are children of God, and what we will be has not yet been made known. But we know that when he appears, we shall be like him, for we shall see him as he is" (1 John 3:2). Also, Paul wrote, "But our citizenship is in heaven. And we eagerly await a Saviour from there, the Lord Jesus Christ, who by the power that enables Him to bring everything under His control, will transform our lowly bodies so that we will be like His glorious body" (Phil. 3:20-21). That final act of God in the heavens will transcend anything I have ever known. Then I will be completely transformed into His image.

Before I meet the Lord, I must attend to the work the Spirit came to do within me, to transform me into the image of His Son. Then I will stand in His presence reflecting the glory of the Only Begotten Son of the Father. My outer being—this temporary framework of flesh and bone—will be suffused with His glory, the final act in this drama will be complete, and all His disciples will enter with Him into His reign over the whole earth (see 2 Tim. 2:12a; Rev. 1:6, 5:10). Finally love, justice, equity, peace, and songs of praise will fill the whole earth, as the Father intended in the beginning.

Chapter Ten

Faith for a Pilgrim

Two Kingdoms

As the years pass I face the growing certainty that I am the citizen of an unseen kingdom whose ruler is the Father who first opened its door to me. Yet I was born into the kingdom of the world whose ruler is the adversary and who is opposed to all I am and do. Within my spirit I sing songs with joy beyond telling, yet I am surrounded by the noises, sounds, cacophonies, strident voices, and tumults of that world which both enthral and distract me. All these paradoxes are part of me as I trust the invisible Lord of that invisible kingdom.

Two kingdoms! Two Lords. Two kinds of relationships. Two sets of principles to daily guide (or dictate) my going out and my coming in. Two ways of life: the way of the flesh and of the world, and the way of faith and of the Spirit. The challenge I face into the twenty-first century is to know the difference and then how to live the difference.

I believe, but even so I encounter another paradox within myself. In place of the promised peace of His kingdom, I so often encounter disturbance of heart and mind. Instead of His joy there is a greyness of soul where no song could ever be sung. I find myself labouring tediously with this world's challenges and failing to enter the rest Jesus promised citizens of His kingdom. I have to conclude that I am failing to live successfully in the world of His Spirit. Both of these failures must be remedied if I am to hear Him say, "well done good and faithful servant" (Matt. 25:21).

Labour and Heavy Laden

Jesus used two Greek words to describe two unsatisfactory experiences I am most familiar with. One can be translated, "labour"; the other can be translated, "heavy laden."

Labour: *kopiao*, "to beat oneself, to exert considerable energy and so be weary, to faint with grief from the effort of it all, having achieved nothing."

Heavy laden: *fortizo*, "to load a person with a burden." These are inner burdens; ill memories that I can't unload, unpleasant relationships I can't sever, knowledge of bad experiences that refuses to go away, obligations I can't meet, guilt and embarrassment because of remembered sins.

The paradox of believing is that I alone am responsible for these burdens and for the experience of being heavy laden, just as I am also responsible for the trust that brings rest in this world of Spirit. I face the Father and trust the Son and my heart rejoices. I face away from Him and I am weary and heavy laden.

Jesus knew about paradoxes in those who believed in Him. He encountered them in Peter who loved Him and had walked with Him for so many miles. I know what it is like to trust Him and yet let the ways of the world intrude; to experience the peace of God following His forgiveness, and yet labour under the burdens of my old nature and of the world.

I have to console myself with the thought that much of my labour and many of the burdens I have borne have come about because of my ignorance. At the early stages in my spiritual walk I never knew any better, and little in what I had been taught helped me find any alternative. I knew about rest, knew it existed, but in those days I had no clue about how to enter the rest that Jesus promised. That must be why Jesus invited His disciples to accept His yoke, to learn of Him and to be at rest.

The Yoke of Learning

Jesus knew the answer to both the labour and the burdens His disciples so often carried. He invites us all to function in one special aspect of His kingdom of Spirit, in the relationship with Him, which transforms our lives into something quite extraordinary. He invited His disciples; "Come unto me all the labouring ones having been burdened and I will rest you. [I like the sound of those last four words.] Take my yoke on you and learn from me because I am meek and lowly in heart and you will find rest to your souls. For my yoke is gentle and my burden is light" (Matt. 11:28–30, literal translation in Greek).

Jesus was using an illustration from farming practice to introduce His disciples to a mystery. They all knew how two draft oxen were yoked together so that the weaker and less skilled of the pair could learn from the stronger who knew how to walk a straight furrow and obey the signals from the ploughman. I believe that the ploughman represents the Father, the stronger ox represents the Lord, and the weaker ox under instruction, represents the disciple.

The yoke was the connection through which two kinds of signals could be sent from the stronger to the weaker. Do what I am doing; and this is the first lesson of obedience to the yoke. Restrain yourself from doing what you are naturally inclined to do; and this is the second lesson of obedience. Some disciples have to work very hard to achieve this kind of success in His kingdom. Others seem to walk this way almost by second nature.

Louise was one of those. She had met the Lord in a time of distress and following her repentance and faith had immediately been filled with His Spirit and with joy. During the following days she would come to our house and we would ask her about her experience of the Lord. Little by little she would reveal what she was learning, principles of faith and obedience that marked a disciple's steady walk with the Lord. When I asked her where she had read that principle in the Scriptures she replied, "Not in the Scriptures! The Lord taught me." The yoke of learning that linked her to the Lord was indeed in place and was working properly.

In Jesus' illustration the weaker ox is required to leave behind its independent patterns of instinct and behaviour that could never be of use in ploughing a straight furrow. I am quite sure that learning the new patterns would never have been easy for the ox (though it certainly was for Louise which makes her experience of faith and of the Spirit all the more remarkable). The weaker ox would have often strained against the restraint of the yoke as it struggled to learn new principle and behaviours. Learning would have required constant repetition until the new patterns the ploughman required became habitual.

Having an independent and wilful nature, I can identify with the wilful weaker ox. Like that animal I have to renounce the old patterns that are disruptive, discordant, and obstacles to growth in the exercise of my trust. I have to let Him guide me in putting them aside. The patterns of an old life are no longer relevant for my walk as His disciple. Under instruction from my Master Teacher, I have to acquire, learn, understand, commit to memory, and practice, practice, practice, until entirely new patterns of thought and obedience have been mastered. They must become automatic; almost instinctive.

I am struck by how patiently the ploughman teaches the weaker ox to live under the yoke and to learn the responses the Ploughman requires. It is by this example that I find His grace.

The Practice of Learning

When I confessed to the Lord, "I believe," and passed through the door into His kingdom, I put myself in the way of learning as a student sitting at the feet of the Master Teacher. The Greek word translated, "learn," is *manthano*. It means: "to learn intellectually from another through personal study and observation of what the teacher says and does." However, learning in theory is not real learning until it has been translated into practice.

Now I encounter an impossibility, two impossibilities in fact. In the first place the yoke is a physical object and there is no way I can be physically yoked with Jesus no matter how I strain the meaning of the words. In the second place I cannot be a

Mary and sit at His feet, much as I would love to. He is gone away. However, Jesus was speaking to disciples of all ages so there has to be another way I can understand this intimate connection with the Master.

The yoke in Jesus' illustration was outer and physical. The yoke that links Jesus and myself together has to be an intimate inner connection of my spirit with His Spirit. I can understand the image of the yoke in no other way. My spirit has been born again through His Spirit. He lives within my reborn spirit. This is the most immediate and intimate relationship; My spirit within His Spirit. His Spirit within me.

Across this inner and most mysterious link—this yoke of spirit to Spirit—instruction flows from Teacher to student. What is my responsibility? Put myself in the way of His instruction by allowing Him and working with Him to identify all those negative and unproductive ideas and behaviours that obstruct effective learning. As part of that obligation I must fasten my inner attention on the Lord and trust Him to teach me.

These words are easy in doctrine, but the practice of the inner yoke between my spirit and His Spirit has never been easy. I know that it is through that Spirit that I have the privilege of immediate access to the words, commands and instruction of the Lord (see John 16:12–15). I have known His commands—they often don't feel like commands—walk this way but not that way, attend to this matter, refuse that inclination, listen to these words, and don't let that insinuation overpower you. Most mysterious of all, it is through that spirit yoke that He forms images within my spirit that testify of what the Lord has for me (those who have had this happen to them will know what I mean).

My challenge is to understand what it means to walk in yoke with the Lord. However, immediately I encounter another paradox. The yoke for the two oxen was the means the ploughman used to control them, but there is no evidence in the Scriptures of the Lord controlling His disciples. Quite the contrary. He knew that Peter would deny Him but He never instructed his errant disciple to stay away from the servant who knew by Peter's accent that he was a Galilean. Nor did the Lord control Paul or Barnabas in their disagreement about the service of John Mark.

To take the paradox a step further, I am the only one who can bring the yoke into effective use. I believe that the moment I trust my Lord unreservedly, without conditions, and obey the instruction to present myself as a living sacrifice to Him the yoke becomes effective. Without that kind of trust and surrender to His Lordship the yoke is an idle implement; my need to learn from Jesus cannot be met, and I will never enter His rest. If I want to please the ploughman, who is the Father, then this can only be because I trust the wiser ox to whom I am yoked (see Heb. 11:6).

The teaching is clear. The yoke of learning, Spirit to spirit, absolves me from independent action. He leads. I follow. So I enter rest which is the cessation of all the labours of my old nature, the making silent all the noisy energies I can generate. They are fruitless unless they are generated by the Spirit through the yoke of learning (see John 15:1–4; Heb. 4:10).

It is a costly lesson to learn that the yoke is linked inextricably with my trust to the Son of the Father. However, it is also permanently linked with the Spirit of the Father. These are three points in a spiritual triangle: my trust in the Lord, the yoke through which I learn, and the work of the Holy Spirit. The first two we have explored. Only one remains to complete this search into what it means to believe—my relationship with the Holy Spirit.

The Holy Spirit

During the last night before His final agonies, Jesus taught His disciples across all ages that the Holy Spirit would teach us all things (John 14:26), remind us of everything Jesus had said (John 14:26), testify about Jesus (John 15:26), guide us into all truth (John 16:13), tell us what is yet to come (John 16:13), and take what belongs to Jesus and make it known to us (John 16:15). I find it hard to imagine a more complete statement of the Spirit's role and the purpose of the inner yoke. If all that Jesus promised that night could be achieved in me as His disciple I would be fulfilled beyond belief.

My challenge is to find out how to relate to this mysterious being who was the agent of creation and who filled and guided Jesus throughout His life. The single name that means more to me than any other is the Greek title Parakletos, Paraclete, "one called to walk alongside the disciple, One called to assist, to admonish, encourage, console, entreat."

The Holy Spirit was there in Jerusalem when the Lord fulfilled His promise that they would be baptised in the Holy Spirit and be filled with power (see Acts 1:5, 8). In the following days He was there filling the disciples as they lived out the amazing days that followed Pentecost (see Acts 4:8, 31).

The Paraclete was there at the meeting of apostles and elders in Jerusalem called to face the problem of Jewish believers who taught that circumcision was necessary for salvation. Following their discussions they wrote, "It seemed good to the Holy Spirit and to us not to burden you with anything beyond the following requirements," which they then spelled out (Acts 15:28). He was also there when Paul on His second missionary journey wanted to go west into the province of Asia and then north into the province of Mysia. Luke reports that the Spirit would not allow them to follow those routes, though we are not told how the Spirit communicated this instruction. Now this same Person is tied to my inner person through the yoke of His eternal Person. Through that yoke all the other promises Jesus made to His disciples about learning may be fulfilled.

How do I relate to this infinite and eternal Person? In Paul's letter to the Galatian assemblies, I find three instructions that complete my search. One instruction is passive and can only be carried out with my cooperation, by the Spirit Himself, but two are active, and responsibility for them lands on my doorstep.

The First Instruction: Be Filled With the Spirit.

Fill: *pleroo*, "to make full, to fill completely, to be complete." I had to remind myself that Paul was not instructing the disciples at Ephesus that they should be half filled with the Spirit or partially filled or made not quite full (see Eph. 5:18). This word tells me that those who are filled with the Spirit are filled completely; no half measures. The same is true of that remarkable statement where Paul defined the standard for being filled with His Spirit, "to know this love that surpasses knowledge—that you may be filled to the [same] measure of all the fullness of God" (Eph. 3:19).

To be filled with the Spirit occurs five times in Luke's record in Acts. Twice it refers to all the disciples gathered together in one place, once to Peter and twice to Paul. I wanted to know what responsibilities these disciples had in this process of being filled so I rang my brother who is a Baptist minister. I can depend on him to get his Greek straight. He confirmed that the words "be filled" were in the passive voice. These disciples were recipients of this divine act. They could not have filled themselves with the Spirit; only the Spirit Himself could fill them.

Perhaps I can draw some meaning from the image of a vessel that is to be filled with water, wine, or oil. It has to be empty and also clean before it can be filled. Nothing else makes sense. If it is not empty and clean then the result will be some kind of mixture when one element is diluted or polluted by another. Of course to my mind there is no way that the Spirit of Christ, who is a person, can ever be diluted or mixed with some inferior substance such as He would inevitably find within my old nature.

Now so much of what I have learned makes sense. I cannot imagine the perfect and Holy Spirit of the Father dwelling in the morass of doubt, fear, and anxiety we have studied, to say nothing of all the desires of my old nature. To my mind there is no way that can happen. First, in submission to Him and in obedience to His inner instructions, I must empty the vessel through the sacrifice of myself to Him, put to death the old man who is opposed to all that the Spirit is and would do, and complete my relationship with Him with unconditional and self-surrendered trust (see

Gal. 5:24).

I sometimes think my life has been like walking in a playground littered with all the throwaway discards of life. When I attempt to walk through the tangle, I stumble, kicking my feet against the garbage I have left there. Or like living in the master living room in my house where I have stored all the junk I have accumulated through my life where desire has been my guiding principle. I want to bring an esteemed guest into that room, but there is nowhere for Him to walk or sit or rest. How do I handle these things?

In answer to my question John was very clear. He wrote, "If we confess our sins, he is faithful and just and will forgive us our sins and purify [cleanse] us from all unrighteousness" (1 John 1:9). The word sin is the translation of the Greek word *hamartia*, which refers to everything I say and do that misses the mark of His righteousness. All the litter in my playground is encompassed by this word. All the junk I have accumulated in my living room misses the mark of His righteousness. What do I have to do with it all? I have to confess it. When I do He is listening to what comes from my heart, as He has so often done. Cleansing follows immediately and the playground and living room are swept clean. His peace is welcomed back into my soul and joy rises like a song born out of the purity that the Spirit brings.

I know from wonderful inner experience that when confession is made, forgiveness and cleansing come as a gift from the Father. In repentance and confession I will have done my part in enabling Him to create that clean inner space where the Lord can dwell, where His Spirit can take His rest and abide safely. Then He can and will express His own nature within me. At that moment He fills me to the brink with His Spirit and His peace and joy follow hard on the heels of His forgiveness. I know I am filled with His Spirit when peace covers and fills me, when joy leaps up in worship, and when I truly am filled with love for Him and for one another. How do I know when I not filled with His Spirit? When these divine gifts are missing from every moment I breathe or when the unruly delinquents of doubt, desire, fear, anxiety, self-condemnation, self-pity, and independence invade my inner space.

I have to confess that there have been countless such moments when through repentance and confession I have moved against the accumulated junk of my life—and of course I go on accumulating it—and I know from a human point of view that there will be countless more such moments. Because I am bound by the sinful nature I inherited from Adam there will always be need for confession.

The Second Instruction: Walk in the Spirit

As soon as I have been filled (or is it refilled?) with His Spirit the responsibility passes to me. Paul instructed the disciples in the Galatian assemblies, "In the Spirit walk and the lusts of the flesh by no means will you perform" (Gal. 5:16, literal translation in Greek). The word walk is *peripateo* from which we get the word peripatetic. On the negative side the term walk refers to the whole round of natural human activities, to every decision I make, to all I say and do, whether alone or in company with other people, in the assembly, in the world, or in every natural waking moment. On the positive side and in relationship with the Holy Spirit, the word "walk" refers to all the thoughts and behaviours that accompany my walking in His Spirit.

I realised that if I didn't want to get wet by walking in the rain I had to walk in the sun. To put it another way, walk in the sun and you will not get wet by the rain. Sunshine is the way of the Spirit. Rain is the way of the flesh. This is only a partial image because the rain is not aggressive and actively opposed to me like the flesh is. That is also what the apostle taught. "For the sinful nature desires what is contrary to the Spirit, and the Spirit what is contrary to the sinful nature. They are in conflict with each other, so that you do not do what you want" (Gal. 5:17). Then it became a little clearer. The Spirit of the Father lives within my reborn spirit. It is not my natural self that was opposed to the flesh. It was my spirit filled and illumined by His Spirit that was contrary to my flesh. My aggressive and independent spirit and flesh, is actively opposed and contrary to His Spirit.

When I let these truths of the Scriptures sink in I realised that Paul was putting two instructions together and so must I. His first instruction: to be filled with His Spirit; and his second instruction: to walk in His Spirit. If I do not take great care to be filled with the joy and peace His Spirit brings, and if His love does not resonate through all my being, then I am a very short step away from walking in the flesh. My walk in His Spirit begins and ends with me being filled with His Spirit.

I find that there is one further outcome of this relationship. Being filled with and walking in the Spirit is tied to how I cope with this inner man who would dictate my motives and lead me—and I acknowledge sadly that it is always with my consent—into dead end streets and alleyways that go nowhere. Paul wrote, "In Spirit walk and the desires of the flesh you will by no means perform" (Gal. 5:16, literal translation in Greek).

The word originally translated "lusts" in the KJV is *epithumia*, and is better translated as "desire which is directed towards anything or person and which attaches itself to that object or person." Many of my wishes are quite benign, such as the plan to purchase a new shirt or weed the garden. However, my desires go beyond such simple plans and purposes.

Desire attaches me to the object of my desire and holds me captive. It locks me onto the desired image whether it is an object I convince myself I must have, a relationship I insist will satisfy my grosser wishes, an achievement beyond my natural abilities, or even a simple activity involving another person.

When I am living in the flesh I won't let any of my desires go and I justify each one with subtle self-serving arguments while I continue to be frustrated when each one is not met. Even when it is met I find myself further tangled in the web of my own deceit and have to justify my sin or what is worse, pretend it doesn't exist. This is quite the opposite of what the Lord intends for His disciples. I am to be filled with the Spirit and then walk in the Spirit so that I may be freed from all the desires that can trap me and hold me captive.

The Third Instruction: Be Led by the Spirit

This desired outcome of believing in Him and being filled with Him has two parts. The first outcome is contained in Paul's injunction, "But if you are led by the Spirit, you are not under law" (Gal. 5:18). The Greek word translated "led" is *ago*, and refers to the Holy Spirit who will, "bear, bring, carry, lead the disciple in the path he should follow." We don't do the leading. He does. How I wish I could claim that He has led me throughout the course of my life. Sadly I cannot. The times I have led myself are beyond counting.

This is another passive verb. He does the leading. I create the conditions within myself so that I can hear what He is telling me about the path He wants to lead me down. When He reveals the path, I submit to His direction. That may involve simply speaking with another in a relationship where grace is the issue, or a life changing decision He leads me to take. I find comfort in both cases, for He not only leads me, as the verb says, He also bears me along and when the going is difficult He carries me and brings me to the conclusion He has marked out for me.

The second part of this humbling experience of being led by the Spirit is found in another verb in that same letter. "Since we live by the Spirit let us keep in step with the Spirit" (Gal. 5:25). The word translated "keep in step" is *stoicheo*, which means, "to stand or go in order, to advance in rows or ranks, to walk according to His rule or order." It is a military term where the one receiving the order is a soldier in the ranks and the one issuing the order is his commanding officer.

I am confounded. Not only do I look for a path for my feet, and that is what I have been taught for most of my walk with the Lord, but I find that He has His own path and knows where He is going in accordance with the Father's will. I am invited to keep in step with the Spirit, to participate in the plans the Father has for His people and for the world.

There is one word of comfort in this. The Spirit is not like the commanding officers I was used to during my military training, bellowing at us to keep in step, get that rifle straight, and to stay in line. Miss a command with them and you will suffer ten laps with a full pack around the parade ground. The Spirit I am glad to say is not like that, though I have to acknowledge that His demands are much more rigorous than the demands of the sergeants who trained us.

At issue with the sergeant was his need to prepare us for some kind of imaginary battle. At issue with the Spirit are the purposes of the Father Himself and those involve redemption, forgiveness, eternal life, grace, the extension of His kingdom, and overcoming the world. I would be most tardy and indeed ignorant and arrogant if I insisted on walking my own way and ignoring these higher purposes, and of course He will call me to account, in the next world if not in this one.

The Final Challenge

I began my discipleship as a pilgrim on a journey, beyond this time and place, to that time and place when I shall see Him face to face. Then His eternal purposes for me and the world, which are the context for my believing, will for the most part have been achieved. It is these same purposes that lead me forward. They call me to a time when my search will be over and I will tie up my vessel at the final wharf and submit my cargo to the Harbour Master.

I trust Him without conditions and without reservations, and in the surrender of myself I allow Him to probe the inner springs of my being and reveal them to me so that I can understand and deal with those things within myself that hinder my trust in Him. I bring my body, soul, and spirit to the One who died and rose again, and submit myself to Him as a sacrifice on the altar of His love and compassion. I enable Him to fill me with His Spirit by having Him sweep clean the playgrounds and storerooms of my life so that He can create in me a fit dwelling place for the Lord of Life. There He will abide in me and I will rest in Him.

To believe is not just a single act. Rather it is the immediate environment of faith in which I have to understand all the intricate details of trusting Him. That environment of faith has many parts, offering my body to Him as a living sacrifice; understanding and resisting the basic principles of this world; being conformed to the image of the Son of the Father; playing my own part in undoing of the terrible heritage of Eden; experiencing the exquisite tenderness of that invisible yoke, and so much more.

Believing introduces me to an eternal panorama of spirit where the Lord sees the past, present, and future, as well as my place in all of it. This spiritual panorama is a little like a vast facsimile of the earthly panorama I saw from Sandakphu, the ridge I climbed separating Nepal and India. This ridge sweeps north and then west and climbs up peak upon peak until the earth is crowned in the west by Everest, the world's highest mountain, and in the north by Kanchenjunga, the world's third highest. Just as my youthful mind was staggered by the vastness and the incredible beauty of that part of His creation, so my older and wiser spirit in union with His Spirit is awed by a panorama of spirit so much more vast and beautiful. One day I may be able to see forever.

For now, looking into the twenty-first century I have two personal challenges. Like Paul writing to Timothy, his son in the faith, I want to be able to say, "I know whom I have believed and I have been persuaded that he is able to guard the deposit of me against that day (2 Tim. 1:12, literal translation in Greek). That is my first challenge.

The second is to look into the times beyond this moment and be able to say, again with Paul, "But one thing I do: Forgetting what is behind and straining toward what is ahead, I press on towards the goal to win the prize for which God has called me heavenward in Christ Jesus" (Phil. 3:13-14).

If I can be found in Him, trusting Him, loving Him, being at rest with His rest, being filled with His Spirit, and being trained and shaped into the image of the Beloved Son who abides within me, I will be content.

We invite you to view the complete
selection of titles we publish at:

www.ASPECTBooks.com

Scan with your mobile
device to go directly
to our website.

Please write or email us your praises, reactions,
or thoughts about this or any other book we publish at:

P.O. Box 954
Ringgold, GA 30736

info@ASPECTBookscom

ASPECT Books titles may be purchased in bulk for
educational, business, fund-raising, or sales promotional use.
For information, please e-mail:

BulkSales@ASPECTBooks.com

Finally, if you are interested in seeing
your own book in print, please contact us at

publishing@ASPECTBooks.com

We would be happy to review your manuscript for free.

www.ingramcontent.com/pod-product-compliance
Lightning Source LLC
Chambersburg PA
CBHW081841170426
43199CB00017B/2804